797,885 Books
are available to read at

Forgotten Books

www.ForgottenBooks.com

Forgotten Books' App
Available for mobile, tablet & eReader

ISBN 978-1-333-44210-1
PIBN 10505043

This book is a reproduction of an important historical work. Forgotten Books uses state-of-the-art technology to digitally reconstruct the work, preserving the original format whilst repairing imperfections present in the aged copy. In rare cases, an imperfection in the original, such as a blemish or missing page, may be replicated in our edition. We do, however, repair the vast majority of imperfections successfully; any imperfections that remain are intentionally left to preserve the state of such historical works.

Forgotten Books is a registered trademark of FB &c Ltd.
Copyright © 2017 FB &c Ltd.
FB &c Ltd, Dalton House, 60 Windsor Avenue, London, SW19 2RR.
Company number 08720141. Registered in England and Wales.

For support please visit www.forgottenbooks.com

1 MONTH OF FREE READING

at

www.ForgottenBooks.com

By purchasing this book you are eligible for one month membership to ForgottenBooks.com, giving you unlimited access to our entire collection of over 700,000 titles via our web site and mobile apps.

To claim your free month visit: www.forgottenbooks.com/free505043

* Offer is valid for 45 days from date of purchase. Terms and conditions apply.

English
Français
Deutsche
Italiano
Español
Português

www.forgottenbooks.com

Mythology Photography **Fiction**
Fishing Christianity **Art** Cooking
Essays **Buddhism** Freemasonry
Medicine **Biology** Music **Ancient Egypt** Evolution Carpentry Physics
Dance Geology **Mathematics** Fitness
Shakespeare **Folklore** Yoga Marketing
Confidence Immortality Biographies
Poetry **Psychology** Witchcraft
Electronics Chemistry History **Law**
Accounting **Philosophy** Anthropology
Alchemy Drama Quantum Mechanics
Atheism Sexual Health **Ancient History**
Entrepreneurship Languages Sport
Paleontology Needlework Islam
Metaphysics Investment Archaeology
Parenting Statistics Criminology
Motivational

THINKING

AN INTRODUCTION
TO ITS HISTORY AND SCIENCE

FRED CASEY

THE LIBRARY
OF
THE UNIVERSITY
OF CALIFORNIA
LOS ANGELES

GIFT OF

Hilde Dietzgen Charlton

In Memory of

Her Mother

THINKING

THINKING

AN INTRODUCTION TO
ITS HISTORY AND SCIENCE

BY
FRED CASEY

1922.
THE LABOUR PUBLISHING COMPANY LTD.
6, TAVISTOCK SQUARE, LONDON, W.C.1

PREFACE

It is hoped that this little sketch of the story of thinking will be of service to those who have neither the time to study or money to purchase the more extensive and expensive works.

Beyond the manner of presentation, the charts,* diagrams and a few opinions at the end of each part, the writer can lay no claim to originality, and since this is obvious, no attempt has been made to give the sources of quotations, as such would only burden the book with references of no practical value to those for whom it is intended. Some of the sources of information taken generally are indicated in the bibliography.

* A print of two charts illustrating the development of the main lines of thought of the principal thinkers from Thales to Marx and Bergson with their names, dates and the chief characteristics of their thinking, for use in connection with Chapters I—VIII, can be obtained from The Plebs Book Department, 162a, Buckingham Palace Road, London, S,W.1. Price 1/-, post free 1 2.

CONTENTS

PART I.
THE HISTORY OF PHILOSOPHY.

CHAP.		PAGE
I	Introduction	11
II	Rise of Greek Philosophy	26
III	Decadence of Greek Philosophy	41
IV	Philosophy in the Middle Ages	51
V	Philosophy from Descartes to Kant	65
VI	The Philosophy of Immanuel Kant	75
VII	Idealism from Kant to Bergson	86
VIII	Materialism from Roger Bacon to Marx	101

PART II.
LOGIC, OR THE SCIENCE OF UNDERSTANDING.

IX	Logic Applied to the General Nature of Thought (Mind) and of Things (Matter)	121
X	Logic Applied to Physical Science	138
XI	Logic Applied to Mental and Moral Problems	152
XII	Various Examples of Applied Logic	170
	Bibliography	187
	Index	189

PART I

THE HISTORY OF PHILOSOPHY

THINKING
ITS
HISTORY AND SCIENCE.

PART I.
THE HISTORY OF PHILOSOPHY.

CHAPTER I*

Introduction

Has the reader ever told a lie? If so, was it right to tell that lie, or better, could it ever be right to lie? It is easy to say people ought not to tell lies, but when deciding about oneself it becomes a most uncomfortable question; we will therefore change the subject by asking a few others of varying character.

What is true democracy?
Would the practice of humanitarian principles be good for society?
Is education good for the working class?
If socialism is bound to come, of what use are social science classes?
Has man a free will?
Why do we say that living things have life?
Why is evil desirable?
Does machine production benefit society?
Is happiness as an end in view morally justified?
Would it be right for socialists to confiscate the property of capitalists, or, is it right to steal?

* See footnote to Preface.

Is it desirable that all people should have good health?

Are strikes unreasonable?

Are majorities always right?

Should workers serve on trade union executives?

The essential character of all these questions—of every question in fact—is contained in the one question what is truth? What is the truth concerning this? What is the truth concerning that? In various ways this great master question has occupied the attention of human beings ever since their brains began to think. In the following chapters it will be our business to briefly review the development of the enquiry. In the last chapter we shall attempt answers to the questions already posed, whilst in the present one we shall prepare our minds for what is to follow. but will first take a look at some fallacious methods employed in endeavouring to arrive at truth.

In places where there is sawdust on the floor and where men go to drink beer, budding politicians can often be heard loudly asking " What did Gladstone say in 1864?" In more refined circles it takes the form of " What did Herbert Spencer say in his 'First Principles'?" In ultra religious circles it is " What did Christ say?" And in some socialist circles " What did Marx say?" Not one of the three latter is any more intellectual than the politician of the " sawdust school," for if a man cannot demonstrate the truth of his propositions " off his own bat," then his appeal to authority is nothing but a demonstration of his own ignorance. Of course the above contains no prejudice against merely quoting a source of information so long as it is not taken as proved without further consideration. Another form of this argument occurs when some person appeals for the acceptance of what he calls his views, on the ground that they are held by millions of people and therefore they are likely to be right. And still another form exists in cases where men claim knowledge because of the length of time they have held certain views, as, for example, in many socialist clubs where men can be heard arguing that they have been members for twelve years and therefore they ought to know what socialism is, whereupon others claim fifteen years and a half and the consequent right to have their views accepted because "they ought to know better."

Another attempted way of arriving at truth, to take an example from the realms of the religious, is to go round to the churches of different denominations, pick out the best from their different teachings, and add them together in a new combination, a sort of "mixed pickles." But, how does a man know what is the best? The same kind of practice is applied to political schools of thought.

Then there are people who say that whatever else we do we ought at least be broadminded, just as though it were possible to be broadminded about such propositions as that two and two make four. In any question broadmindedness is, as a matter of fact, only a superfine name for ignorance, for men do not suspend action because they suspend judgment, so in the end, being broadminded amounts to them acting without knowledge.

A species of broadmindedness more particularly relating to the question of whether there is or is not a God, appears under the name of Agnosticism. Apart from the inconsistency of contemplating at one and the same time two possibilities each of which contradicts the other, in practice agnostics never by any chance act as though there was a God, which in reality proves them to be materialists who at bottom believe there is no God, though in the face of the dominant respectability of present-day society, many are too cowardly to admit it.

Then again, some people rely upon common sense just as if common sense was bound to be right, and this quite regardless of the fact that in different localities different aspects of common sense prevail.

Returning to the question of truth: there is no need to suggest that all persons are "strangers to the truth," for if they did not know when they were right they could never tell when they were wrong; so no great harm will be done by applying a test. If every reader will put the above questions to a dozen friends, separately, he will not get exactly the same answers to every question from every person. Under such circumstances how will he know which is right? for evidently two different answers to the same question cannot both be true. This leaves us just where we were. We are still seeking truth, as the old Greeks were two thousand six hundred years ago. Truth is only another name for knowledge, or wisdom, and the Greek word for wise is " sophos."

Now, how much of this wisdom do we possess, how much do we really know? We are all acquainted with the old saying "seeing is believing," so let us tackle the problem from that standpoint. Take a piece of board, two feet square and half an inch thick, say a small drawing-board; if this is held at arm's length it gives us the impression of a square, but if we turn it part way round, like a half-open door, we see an oblong; if we continue turning it goes narrower, until it gives us the impression of a straight line half an inch wide. What shape is it? Square, of course, because we saw it that way first. But suppose we had seen it the other way first, would it in that case not be square? Moreover, if a lighted spirit lamp be placed between us and the board, but low down so that it heats the air between ourselves and the board, the straight edges of the board appear as wavy lines. Again, if we see it through a child's telescope, with the small lens nearest the board, it will appear to be smaller. Or a person troubled with astigmatism (a faulty curvature of the lens of the eye) may see it with some edges blurred, or out of focus, whilst others are sharp. The shape of the board, then, depends upon its position in relation to ourselves, our eyes, and the condition of the air or other medium through which we see it; and since this shape varies with different persons, or with variations in the combination of other factors, how can we say which is the true shape?

Or consider its colour. Let us agree that the board

is a nice light-brown when held in sunlight, if a shadow is cast on some part of it, this part will be a darker shade than the rest, or in a dark room the board will have no colour at all; so how can we tell which is its true colour?

Ah, well; if seeing is not believing, surely feeling should give us a better foundation. Let us try. Is the board hard or soft? It is hard when we feel with our fingers but soft if we feel with a woodworker's chisel, so in itself we cannot say that it is truly hard Is it heavy? It is heavy to a young child but light to a strong man. Is it solid? It is solid if we try to push our fingers though it but it cannot stop X-rays, or, given sufficient time, water would pass through it, therefore we cannot say whether the board is truly heavy or truly solid, for merely feeling at it gives us no clue.

The foregoing, of course, does not exhaust our problems by any means. As another example we might ask how can three individuals be at the same time one individual? How can *many* be *one?* If we say that an individual man is such because he is part of mankind, then mankind is the unit and each individual man is a part of that unit, consequently the part is only a fraction and not a complete individual. Again, the universe remains the same universe and yet it is constantly changing; how can that be? Or, if it be said that the universe does change because its parts are changing, **what possibility is there of any truth at all?** And yet, there must be truth somewhere if we could only find it; at least so it seemed to the Ancient Greeks who were the first to occupy themselves systematically with such questions. They realised they did not possess truth, but they were longing for it, they " loved truth for its own sake," and sought it irrespective of consequences. They were accordingly lovers of truth, and the Greek word for loving is " philos," wherefore putting " philos " and " **sophos** " together we see how the men who among them sought truth, were " lovers of wisdom " or " philosophers."

In those days a philosopher was a person who sought

truth in any field of enquiry, astronomy, mathematics, logic, ethics; though as time went on certain branches of knowledge became specialised, as, for example, theology, and later different sciences, such as chemistry, geology, botany, astronomy, mathematics, physics, psychology, and many others, so that in modern times philosophy is left with such questions as the relation of the one to the many, the essential or underlying natures of matter, of mind and of life; the existence of God, the question of free will, the question of a future life, the relation between mind and matter, or as it is called, between " thinking " and " being," and it will be our business in succeeding chapters to follow, in outline, the development of the enquiry from its beginning in the Greek colony in Asia Minor, approximately six hundred years before Christ, up to the present time, and to show the positive results achieved; but since thinking cannot be understood without reference to the material conditions governing the lives of the thinkers during any given period, it will be useful, briefly, to review the material conditions that preceded and ultimately made possible that branch of thinking we now know as philosophy.

In the illimitable space we call the sky there are thousands of enormous masses of matter greater than our earth flying about at speeds of anything approaching twenty miles a second. They are cold and dark, but when two of these meet they smash each other into atoms, and their motion is converted into a frightful heat. They become a vast white-hot cloud or nebula of fine particles, millions of miles in extent. This nebula begins to contract, and part of the heat is given off; but the contraction, by the friction of the particles, causes a still greater heat in the interior, so that as the body becomes more condensed it assumes a character that we might faintly imagine by thinking of a mass of molten iron, though immensely more so. Such intense heat breaks up even the atoms into their basic " strain centres " or electrons. With the uneven condensation of such an irregularly shaped body it begins to turn round, and as it increases the spinning motion, it throws off great portions of itself. It is supposed that our sun was at one time a body of this kind, and that our earth is one of the portions thrown off spinning into space. The earth then was originally a ball of fiery matter, and its story from that time is essentially one of cooling, and the consequences following from that cooling.

As the heat passed away through space, the different systems of electrons settled into their peculiar atoms, such as oxygen, hydrogen, carbon, etc., which act and re-act on one another, and which existed as gases forming an atmosphere round the central molten mass. In time the melted matter cooled so much that it formed a skin or crust on the outside. With further cooling the oxygen and hydrogen combined to form water which as it rained down on the central mass was rapidly driven off in the form of steam, only to condense and come down again to repeat the process, a process which, of course, hastened the cooling of the general body, and resulted in forming an ocean surrounding the greater part of the globe. So now there were three layers of matter surrounding the molten centre—a crust of rock, a layer of water and an atmosphere of gases.

But the centre had not gone to sleep; the titanic inside forces were in opposition to the contracting crust of rock, and as the crust cracked, large masses of it were thrust upward out of the water. This naturally redistributed the pressure on the centre, and since the oxygen and hydrogen that formed the water was now taken out of the atmosphere, the atmosphere lost its former enormous pressure (estimated at 5,000 lbs. to the square inch), consequently such land as there was above water tended to increase until it formed a huge continent surrounding the northern hemisphere. Torrents of rain wore the high parts of the land away, and as tons of sediment settled on the lower levels and on the floor of the ocean this increased pressure made large tracks of land sink while it forced others higher out of the water, and in some cases actually bent the surface upward in huge wrinkles, thus forming chains of mountains. In this way that part of the northern land that is now the bed of the Atlantic Ocean was forced under water, and similarly were stretches of land from Africa to Brazil and from Africa to Australia also lost, while Africa and South America took their present form. The re-distribution of land and water, the purifying of the atmosphere through the plants consuming the carbon dioxide, the forming of great lakes and the forcing of great tracts of land up into the colder atmosphere, all tended to bring about important climatic changes resulting in immense sheets of ice which, as they shifted, scarred and tore the surface of the land, and, as they melted, formed rivers, channels and lakes. All these changes had a great deal to do with the forms of living things that for thousands of years had dwelt on the earth, so we must now go back to follow their evolution.

Just as it is normal under certain conditions for gunpowder to explode, or a match to burn, so is it normal for matter in certain other combinations to exhibit the phenomena we call life. Accordingly life is not a thing, but a function. "When did living things first appear? Where did they come from? What was their character? Frankly, we do not know." The many different combinations of matter had been evolving from the time of the firemist, or nebula, so there is evidently no point at which we could say when a certain combination was living. We therefore arbitrarily select the point when minute specks of the combination called protoplasm (the known physical basis of all living things) were formed, and lived individual lives millions of years ago in the original ocean. These specks of jelly, about one-thousandth of an inch in diameter, were the parent stock from which both plants and animals developed. Among very low organisms it is exceedingly difficult to tell which are plants and which are animals, the points being much disputed, but it is usual to call them plants if they take their food from the chemicals of the air, water, or land, and convert these into protoplasm, and to call them animals if they take ready-made protoplasm as their food, that is, if they live on plants or other animals.

If the organism feeds on air, water, etc., it has no need to move or to develop organs of sense, except to a very limited extent, so it becomes rooted and stays where it is; but the organism that lives on other organisms must go and find them, or follow them, or at least develop limbs for catching them as they come near, and so it develops the necessary organs of sense which enable it to respond to its environment; accordingly we got the two divisions of living things, plants and animals. Plants passed through various stages, from the green matter that we see clinging to a rainspout, through sea-weeds, ferns, flowers with sex organs, and an immense variety up to the monster trees of the Coal Age (estimated at from twenty to twenty-eight million years ago). In the sea, animals existed at this time in great numbers and variety, as the result of an evolution from the lower forms. There were amœboids, or single-celled animals, then clusters of cells that double in on themselves, forming stomachs. Higher in the scale some cells specialise as germ or sex cells, and some become especially sensitive; the latter are gathered together in the head and ultimately become brains that are connected with the organs of sense; the digestive cells line the stomach, while other cells develop the functions of locomotion, excretion, etc. Some animals, such as sponges, corals, etc., attached themselves to the floor of the ocean and developed suckers or arms for catching unwary swimmers; others swam about in search of food, preying on one another, and it is the evolution of the latter branch through the forms of fishes, reptiles, birds and mammals that lead up to man.

Long before the Coal Age, animals up to the level of the fish had existed in the sea, but there were no land animals such as we know, because they could not have existed until the plants had freed the atmosphere from carbon dioxide—a food for plants but a poison for air-breathing animals. As the struggle for life became more intense with every increase in numbers, and particularly as the re-formation of the land had resulted in enclosed lakes from which there was no escape to the open sea, the hunted ones made their escape by taking to the land, the swimming bags of the fishes being converted into lungs and their fins into feet. These amphibia later became reptiles of enormous size, though with exceedingly small brains. Ultimately the giants perished through lack of food when parts of the earth became very cold and ice-bound; again it was a question of escape to warmer climes, and it was the swifter, most intelligent, warm-blooded and smaller animals (those requiring least food) that survived. Once again, for escape as numbers increased, the web-footed leaping lizards took, as it were, to swimming in the air, and so developed into birds, while another type of reptile developed mammary glands by which the young could be fed from the mother after birth. This latter evolution is supposed to have taken place on the now lost continent between Africa and Brazil. These part-reptile part-mammal creatures had a coat of hair to keep them warm, and four-chambered hearts to supply richer and warmer blood to their bodies; due to this, and the anxieties of existence, they developed a brain capacity beyond what had been before. There were many species of them, all belonging to the lowest class of mammals, and they gradually overran the earth, so that from one or other all the present-day varied types of animals have been evolved. One of the latter types, the lemur, about the size of a cat, and assumed to have been evolved on the lost Afro-Asian continent, is supposed to be the common ancestor of monkeys, apes and men. The fore feet of lemurs developed into hands with which they climbed into the trees where they lived. It is supposed that this development of hands afforded scope for the development of brains, since it enabled their possessors to undertake many activities denied to other animals; and it is further conjectured that tree climbing led eventually to an upright posture as found in man. Man has therefore

THINKING

been evolved from the lemur, through an ape stage, though not from any existing ape; the apes are his cousins, that is all.

The home of the ape-men, probably a million years ago, was south of Asia; from that time onwards the story is one of increasing intelligence or capacity of brain functioning, and *increasing ability in the making of tools*. They lived in caves or trees, with no language or religion, no knowledge of how they came to be born, nor any knowledge of what we mean by death. They used sharp flints as choppers; they discovered the use of fire probably from the sparks of iron ore; they began to live in communities for purposes of defence, and gradually emerged from their state of savagery into the barbarian stage. During this stage, religious practices came into being, also the spoken language; written language began with drawings on the borders of caves and on rocks. Religious practices arose through ignorance regarding natural forces, such as thunder, lightning, germinal forces, and so on; abstract things, such as Springtime, came to be personified and reckoned as gods. Understanding death as merely a longer duration of sleep, they had no idea of anything but life, consequently with them dead men had simply gone to live in the immortal regions, and from dreams they got their ideas of the immortal interior. A combination of religious belief and spoken language produced the later mythologies and legends of gods, devils, immortal life, heaven, virgin births, and so on. All this time the development of tools was having its effect in so far as with newer and better tools it was possible to accumulate a store of food, which rendered it unnecessary to wander about in search of it; but, to pass from barbarism to civilisation, with an ordered and centralised government, needed something besides mere hand tools. Peace, in which to develop social organisation, along with a continuous supply of food in one locality, are the two primary essentials for civilisation, and we have now to see the reasons why the first civilisation took place in Egypt.

Since animals live on plants or other animals, their

basic food is vegetable. Vegetation depends upon the presence of moisture, ultimately rain, and a given rainfall depends upon the direction of moisture-carrying wind, which again depends on many geographical factors, such as the existence of mountains. A continued supply of food depended accordingly on a certain combination of material conditions. Where those conditions enabled barbarians to get the necessaries of life with a lesser expenditure of energy than formerly, energy was saved for other purposes; *in this lies the essential character of progress.* Now those tribes that lived in places accessible to other tribes, and which were therefore open to attack, had to expend a great deal of energy in defence; accordingly, those who were naturally protected by the sea, deserts, mountain ranges, and so on, stood the best chance of becoming civilised, and nowhere were those conditions so complete as in Egypt along the valley of the Nile, which is protected on the east and west by deserts, partly so on the south, and by the sea on the north. The warm winds from the west bring their moisture from the Atlantic across the great Sahara desert; they are turned upward by the high lands south of Egypt, whereupon they lose their grip of the moisture, which rains down on the gathering grounds of the river Nile, in central Africa and Abyssinia. South of Assuam there is a great tract of sandstone which, being comparatively soft, has been worn by the river into very deep gorges from which the water cannot spread, consequently nothing will grow for any distance on either side; but north of Assuam the base is hard limestone, in which the river has first worn a valley approximately ten miles wide, and has covered this with soil brought down with the floods from the Abyssinian mountains. These floods occur periodically, which circumstance constitutes another important factor in our story of civilising conditions, for in tropical countries one day is very like another the whole year round, so there is no necessity to provide for the future, but outside the tropics there are seasonal changes, more and more severe with approach to temperate regions, and these changes necessitate provision for the bad periods, but such provision cannot be satisfactorily carried out without some centre of authority. Here accordingly were the kind of soil, the moisture, the peaceful conditions, and the necessity of making provision for the future which implies a centralised directive administration, which conditions, taken altogether, are necessary for barbarians to develop into civilised men. The development took a very long time, in all probability some thousands of years before the period of those whom we call the Ancient Egyptians, and the latter date from about 4500 B.C.

The next most likely set of conditions existed in Mesopotamia, between the rivers Euphrates and Tigris, with Babylon as the centre; but without outlining them here, it will be sufficient for our purpose to point out that those two peoples were kept apart by the Syrian desert. The Babylonians were subject to invasions of Semitic tribes which from time to time surged out of Arabia, a high land with a singularly pure air, whose inhabitants bred in numbers out of all proportion to the means of feeding them, so they went out in great hordes to the lands " flowing with milk and honey," and became more or less absorbed and civilised. But while the two principal civilisations were, in the beginning, kept apart by the Syrian desert, a few thousand years of tool development wrought a change; they had tamed and domesticated animals for working and for transport, invented new weapons in response to the wandering Semitic invaders, they could produce more wealth of certain kinds than they needed for their own use, and could afford to trade with it, they could produce an abundant supply of food that could be carried on pack animals; with all this, travel, trading and war, on an ever increasing scale, became possible. But the Syrian desert was still impassable for regular intercourse, therefore the easiest way was what became the great north road from Egypt across the Sinai desert, up through Syria, round the top of the great desert, and down the Euphrates valley. Over these roads many wars were fought, the Jews in Palestine ultimately getting crushed and scattered.

But there were also other tribes from farther north and east, Assyrians, Medes and Persians, who fought and traded in these parts, so that the whole region now known as the Near East became the centre of conflicting civilisations whose trade was constantly being pushed north-west into Asia Minor and along its southern shore. Meanwhile the Phoenicians who lived along the coast of Western Syria, with ideas of river boats originally brought from the Euphrates, had tackled the problem of the sea and had traded along the north of Africa to Carthage and other places; they came in conflict with Greeks, who were also a seafaring people. Persia had in the later times become the dominant power of the then civilised world; she had already colonised a great part of Asia Minor and developed trade all along its southern shore, as well as in the Ægean Sea; she represented the East pushing out to conquer the West. But the Greeks had also done some colonising in Asia Minor; they were warlike on sea as well as on land, and had ideas of the conquest of Persia; they represented the West out to conquer the East, and naturally the conflict in war followed the paths of the conflict in trade because there lay the roads for men to travel; consequently it is along those paths we should expect to find the greatest conflict of ideas or thinking. Along those trading routes were, for those times, great cities, one of which, called Miletus, was situated at the mouth of the river Meander, in the south-west of Asia Minor, and here lived Thales, who came of a high Phoenician family, and who is regarded as the earliest of Greek philosophers; he might be represented as the western spear-head of the scientific thinking of his day, piercing the thousands of years' old religious traditions of the east.

ABSTRACT. From even such an exceedingly general outline as the present, a thoughtful reader will be able to gather that just as life is a function of certain combinations of naturally evolved matter, so is thinking a function of naturally evolved special parts of that matter—organs of sense and brains; thereafter thinking depends upon the material relations between animals and the rest of nature. Accordingly, since men, the animals with hands, possess the capacity for making tools by which they modify the relations between themselves and nature, they consequently *by those means modify their thinking,* for in proportion as better tools led to increased production and consequent trading, so did trading develop a wider type of society, and so were strangers thrown more and more into contact with each other. With regard to religious thought, not only they but their different gods also came into conflict; this, along with other factors, led eventually towards the idea of one God. We have seen that animals, apart from man, evolve along biological lines, but the factor of tool development necessitates changes in man's social relations so that man evolves sociologically. The changes in social relations reflect themselves in thinking and appear as customs, laws, religions, philosophies and sciences. Trading, for example, required standards of measurement in exchanging quantities of goods (arithmetic), also methods of measuring land and roads (geometry), the navigation of the sea, and dozens of other things; but just as changing material conditions led their thinking in a scientific direction, so did this thinking come in conflict with the unscientific superstitions and religious explanations of all things supposed to have been got direct from the gods. All things were recognised to be constantly changing, but since they did not come from nothing, or pass into nothing, it was thought that some one substance must be the base of all things, and it is the merit of the ancient philosophers to have begun the search for that one thing which remained permanent through all its changing forms, or in other words, to have begun the search for universal rock-bottom truth.

CHAPTER II

Rise of Greek Philosophy

Newer tools brought trading. Trading brought war in which prisoners were made into slaves. From being the common property of a tribe, the tools became the private property of individuals, and, through the private ownership of the products, led to the forming of social classes with different inner classes and castes, the whole divided broadly into masters and slaves. This had happened long prior to the rise of Greece, therefore the glories of Greek architecture, literature, statecraft, philosophy, etc., were the outcome of a mode of production where slaves performed the work; nor could they have come into being without slavery. Of course, when speaking of the Ancient Greeks we never mean the slaves, without whose work the culture could never have taken place, nevertheless it is true that philosophers could not live on mere learning, they must have been provided for by somebody, so evidently chattel slavery was the economic basis of a great social advance; it produced its particular types of thinking, and so far as philosophy is concerned we must now consider the chief doctrines of the exponents of that thinking.

As indicated in the last chapter, the beginning of philosophical enquiry is associated with the name of THALES (born about 636 B.C., of Miletus) who imagined the one universal substance to be water—the blood of animals is watery, plants cannot exist without water, even "dry" land contains a percentage of water, and so on. He was a philosopher because he sought essential truth; this is his merit, his actual work otherwise was of no use. He was a naturalist because he turned to natural substances in his investigations.

ANAXIMENES (c. 560-480 B.C., of Miletus) thought he had found the universal essence in air—our souls were composed of air or spirit. Therefore from a natural and sensuous thing he derived the infinite; water was for him limited, it was too coarse, but in air, which we feel though do not see, we have a finer thing that pervades all things (ether).

ANAXIMANDER (born about 610 B.C., of Miletus) declared that an unlimited and infinite substance was the essence of all things, but did not say what it was; he did not define it as any one thing, such as air or water, but merely spoke of it as the principle of all change, of all becoming and passing away; it was "that" out of which worlds and gods arise and into which they ultimately return. It was immortal, had no beginning and would never pass away; it therefore contained everything within it, or rather was everything in continuity.

HERACLITUS (576-480 B.C., of Ephesus, a city a little north of Miletus) thought the moving spirit of all things was fire (not flame—more properly heat, the principle of fire), but since fire or heat was constantly changing there was not even one thing in the universe that did not change; this was, of course, rather awkward for those who wanted to find something permanent.

PYTHAGORAS (6th century B.C., of Samos, an island off the coast of Asia Minor, not far from Miletus and Ephesus, afterwards settled at Crotona in S. Italy) conceived the essential nature of things to be number. The universe is "one," but so is every single part "one." Combinations of parts, no matter how many, become "one," for example, the number of pages in a book, or the number of vibrations in a musical note and the number of beats in its duration; "one" is the beginning of all things, the starting point in all calculations. Had he used this idea symbolically, as arithmetic is used to-day, it would have been intelligible, but according to G. H. Lewes, on the authority of Aristotle, he went on to suppose that number was the *essence of things.*

Pythagoras was the founder of mathematics, the discoverer of proportion in musical harmony, and the founder of a religious sect in Crotona where he taught the immortality and transmigration of souls.

ANAXAGORAS (500-418 B.C., of Clazomenæ in Lydia, the centre of S.W. Asia Minor; afterwards went to Athens) taught that everything existed from eternity, but that things were separate and not in continuity as with Anaximander. They were originally all mixed up, but have been and are continually being sorted out, as time goes on, by intelligence which sees in them their distinct and useful qualities; wherefore since useful things can not be such without, apparently, an intelligent appreciation of them, we see the essential nature of all things to be due to Mind or Intelligence. In this way he reduced the many *kinds* of things (they had all existed through all time) serving different purposes, and usually referred to as "the wonderful order in the universe," to the one primary motion or cause (not a moral guidance). "The Infinite Intelligence was the architect of the Infinite Matter." Mind was the *one* moving spirit that fashioned or arranged the *many* material phenomena, but, as other philosophers complained, he did not show the *connection* between the one and the many, or, we might say, did not explain the nature of the one by reference to the different purposes served by the many, a doctrine known as "teleology."

PARMENIDES (born c. 536 B.C., of Elea, now called Velia, in S. Italy) made a decided distinction between thoughts obtained through reason and those obtained through the senses. Since the senses showed him a world wherein all was change, thoughts got in that way could at best be only opinions, because we never could say "for certain." But in addition to those he had certain convictions that he felt were true; the latter thoughts, which according to him were produced by "reason alone," led him to the conclusion that in truth nothing changed, for all the seeming change was only illusion.

ZENO (c. 490-435 B.C., of Elea, and afterwards Athens), a pupil of Parmenides, in defending his master's apparent contradictions, invented the method of argument known as "dialectics," which consists in showing the error in a statement by reducing it to absurdity through questioning and cross-questioning, with the object of ultimately arriving at truth. He propounded several puzzles, of which the following may be taken as a type: a stone when thrown a distance comes *at the end* to a state of rest, but before it reaches the end it has to pass the middle; as this middle is *the end* of a shorter distance, the stone is at rest there also, and similarly since every point is an end, whether it is called middle or not, the stone is really at rest all the time, although it seemed to move. By such arguments Zeno attempted to prove that motion could not take place, so, amongst all the change going on in the universe, both he and his master taught that nothing changed, for motion was impossible.

At this time, and for a considerable period afterwards, Athens was the "hub of the universe," and the chief city in Greece. Greece was not a country governed from one centre, as England is governed from London, but was composed of separate city states, each with its own government and laws to suit itself. As already mentioned, the Greeks had colonised parts of S.W. Asia Minor, whose coast-land was called Ionia. The philosophers belonging to this region form the Ionian school; those coming from Miletus being sometimes spoken of as the Milesian school. The reader will remember that these philosophers had sought truth in natural objects, such as water, air, etc.; they were, therefore, naturalists or physicists. Southern Italy had also been colonised, and its philosophers of course form the Italian school, one portion of which is referred to as the Eleatic, because its chief representatives were natives of Elea. But while the Ionians were physicists, the Italians (Pythagoras, Parmenides, Zeno, etc.) had developed along abstract lines, and had sought truth by mathematical and dialectical reasoning, that is, by leaving nature alone and relying entirely on their minds. The beginning of this abstract inquiry might be traced back to the "Mind" of Anaxagoras, or even to the "Infinite" of Anaximander. There were therefore two types of thinking in the physicists on the one hand, and the mathematicians or dialecticians on the other. Athens was, of course, the great centre of attraction for all Greeks, and when, in course of time, Zeno arrived there, the dialectical line of enquiry came into conflict with the physical. This conflict resulted in establishing dialectics as the correct method to be used in philosophic enquiry, which means that philosophers must turn away from nature and solve their problems by argument, that is, by thought alone; it also led to the creation of the Sophists and Sceptics.

The Sophists were, as their name implies, men of knowledge, or at least they were regarded as such by those who paid to learn from them. They travelled from city to city teaching for a living, but they were dialecticians who could prove anything to be right if it suited them, just as a barrister might with superior argument plead successfully for the life of a murderer. Travelling about, they found in different cities different laws in relation to different conditions; what was right in one place was wrong in another. To them there was no absolute truth, so it was no use attempting to teach definite systems of knowledge; they taught accordingly the art of rhetoric in pleading any cause, but particularly in politics and law, because there being no real truth, one opinion is as good as another, and those persons are likely to come best off who most cleverly understand and use the art of persuasion. They were the Relativists of their time, but this relativity must not be identified with modern relativity, it was only "the protest of baffled minds." The Sophists came to be regarded as dishonest reasoners who knew they could prove nothing but were all along pretending to do so. The Sceptics were at least honest, they knew they could prove nothing and said so, nevertheless this put them in a worse position than the Sophists, if, indeed, it could be called a position, for no thinking man can rest content with nothing; they were the Agnostics of their time, their numbers developed as time went on, so that eventually they practically killed philosophy in Greece. We shall refer to them later.

It is said that Greek philosophy, properly speaking, begins with SOCRATES (469-399 B.C., of Athens), inasmuch as he, the son of a sculptor, who frequented any place where men gathered together, there to argue with anybody who would, so developed the art of dialectics as to make of it a new method of enquiry in philosophy. He was very severe on the Sophists who had no basis of truth, and by his merciless questioning brought out the idea that if one thing was right under some conditions, another thing under others, and so on, this could only be on the assumption that there was a " right " that remained permanently right *independently of how men thought,* and consequently it was the business of a philosopher to employ dialectics in order to discover the essential and permanent natures of such things as rightness, justice, honesty, bravery, love, etc., and to define those natures in such a way that they might be generally understood and accepted as moral standards for all men; first define and then deduce, *in this we can see the beginning of logical system.*

This concept, of the *permanence of a certain inner nature* which could not be grasped by the senses but by the understanding alone, although only applied to morality by Socrates, was afterwards more widely applied by Plato and became the keynote of his whole teaching. Meanwhile it was the first step towards elaborating ethics as a science, so we see one branch of philosophy gradually turning away from the problem of the nature of existence to that of conduct, or what should men do in order to do right, or again, what should be the aim in life. From this side of Socrates' teaching flow two schools of thought—the Cyrenaic, so named from Cyrene, the native place of Aristippus its chief exponent, and the Cynic with Antisthenes as its leader.

ARISTIPPUS (430-360 B.C., of Cyrene in Africa) was influenced by the Sophists as to the impossibility of arriving at the truth of anything, because since each person judges according to his impressions, no one can be trusted to judge correctly; but he was also influenced by Socrates, who had dwelt much on the permanent nature of The Good. Aristippus thought the greatest good was to be found in pleasure, but for the attainment of constant pleasure one must not overdo the thing, therefore a moderate pleasure was the best aim in life.

ANTISTHENES (c. 445-370 B.C., of Athens) studied under the Sophists, and even established a school, but afterwards took both himself and his students to learn from Socrates. He became captivated by the idea of the moral perfection of man; this impulse he got from Socrates, but never took to the method of Socrates, and consequently was one-sided.

In his pursuit of moral perfection he adopted the simple life, but carried it to extremes. He made a god of poverty, and ostentatiously paraded it. He was a man of gloomy temper and snarling ways, and it is said that the name Cynic (the Greek name for dog) was given to him and his followers because they lived the lives of dogs. According to him the best aim in life was to attain the virtues of moral perfection by casting away all the comforts of easy living that might interfere with the development of our moral natures, and his followers went to such an extent as to ignore not only life's comforts, but even its ordinary decencies. Diogenes, who lived and died in the streets, was probably the best known member of this school.

The other side of Socrates' teaching was the more truly philosophic in that it clung to the search for that permanent something which abides through all the changes of its parts. This line of thought, as already indicated, was taken up and developed by PLATO (427-346 B.C., of Athens).

Aristocles, surnamed Plato (the broad-browed or broad-shouldered), was of an illustrious line; on the maternal side he was connected with Solon (c. 638- c. 558 B.C.), the great Greek statesman, and, as with many great names, he was the subject of fable; for instance, he was said to be the child of Apollo and a virgin. Well educated, and skilled in gymnastics, he competed in the great games. He learned dialectics from Socrates, but was previously acquainted with Cratylus who, as a follower of Heraclitus, taught that all things changed therefore no truth could be stated. Plato found no satisfaction in this, although it was true that *all things that appeared to his senses* did indeed change.

In the teaching of Anaxagoras he found the idea of a *universal mind;* in that of Parmenides the idea of a *permanent and unchanging* universe; from the followers of Pythagoras he learned of the immortality of souls; but it was from Socrates he got the chief clue to his doctrine. Socrates had taught the permanent moral natures of rightness, justice, honesty, and the like. Plato carried this farther and imagined real permanent natures of all other things, both abstract and concrete, such as straightness, equality, men, animals, etc. All the individuals of any one species were, so to speak, more or less perfect, though perishable, copies or imitations of their genus or essential natures. For the purpose of explaining, we might imagine the permanent nature of man to be a pattern from which individual men were made, or, that individual men partook more or less of the perfection of the pattern which existed in reality on its own account. With Plato this general nature or pattern was not a mere thought, it existed whether we were aware of it or not, it could not be seen with the eyes, nor indeed grasped by any of the senses, it could only be understood. Each separate species had its own general nature, which Plato called its Form or Idea; in those days the word " idea " did not mean a thought in the mind as it does with us. With a further extension he conceived all the different Forms to be

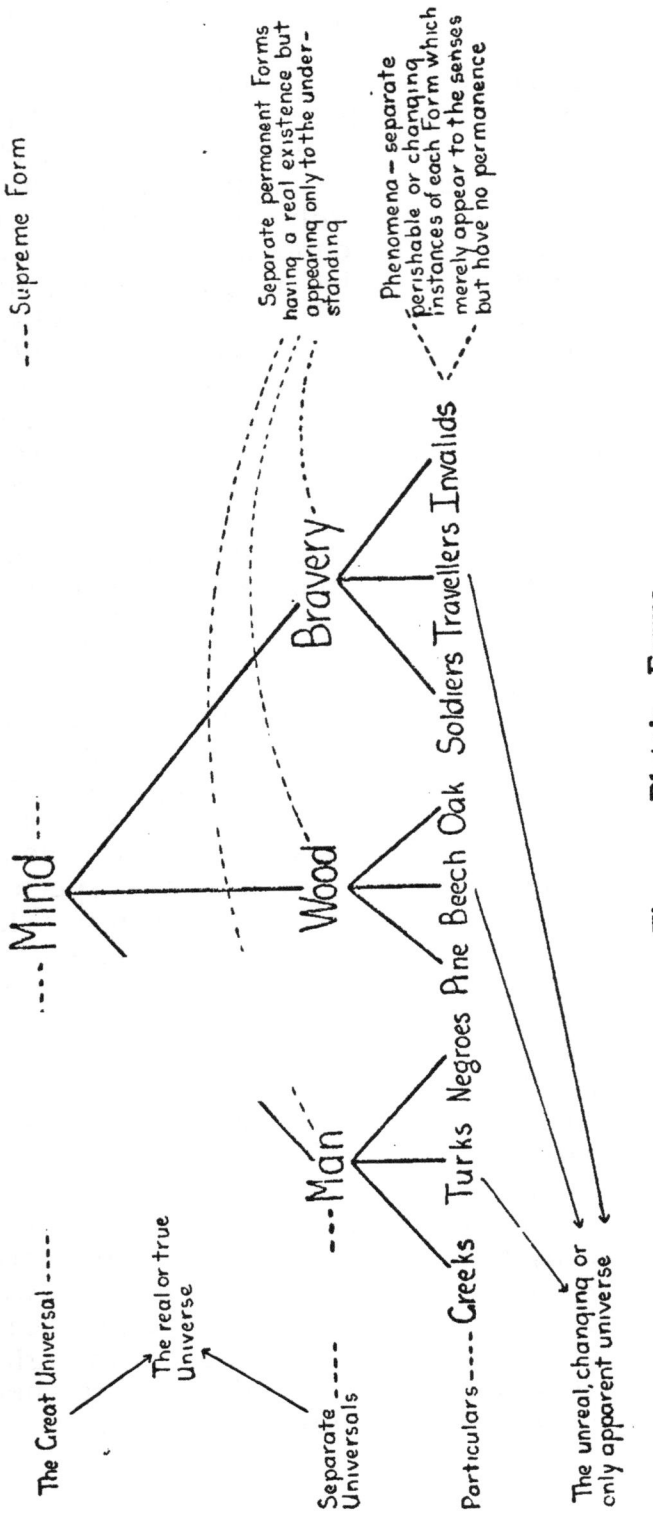

Fig. 1. Plato's Forms

parts of one universal Form, the Supreme Mind or Intelligence—the Soul of the World. Fig. 1 may serve to make this clear. This Soul of the World, or Universal Intelligence pervading the world, was that permanent truth which was the goal of philosophy, it was the one in relation to the many.

Since only what satisfies the intelligence can be regarded as real, and since only philosophers who possess a high degree of intelligence can apprehend reality, so, in Plato's opinion, ought the rulers of communities to be philosophers, and so was he led to write the " Republic," a utopia in which he outlined the training necessary to provide the State with such rulers.

" He had a small house and garden a mile or so from Athens, and near the Academy, or garden adjoining the sacred precincts of Hecademus. Here there were shady walks, and a gymnasium, where he founded his school of philosophy, which for centuries was known as the Academy," and it was here that Aristotle, one of the greatest thinkers of Greece, studied as a young man.

ARISTOTLE (384-322 B.C., of Stagira, on the west coast of what is now the Gulf of Contezza, in northern Greece) was the son of a physician who died leaving him at the age of seventeen his own master, young, ardent, ambitious and rich. He was slender in person, had delicate health, but was an astonishing brain worker. He went to Athens, where he remained about twenty years, studying, and writing on a vast number of subjects—Ethics, Rhetoric, Logic, Poetics, Zoology, Comparative Anatomy, Psychology, Physics, Astronomy, etc., so there can be no attempt made to do justice to his work in such a brief outline as the present. He was disliked by certain political leaders, who accused him of blasphemy, inasmuch as he had paid homage to mortals by raising statues in memory of his friend Hermias and to his wife Pythias. He escaped from Athens and retired to Chalcis, but after Plato died, returned to find Xenocrates teaching in the Academy, so obtained permission to teach morning and evening in the Peripatos or shady walks of the Lyceum, the finest of Athens' gymnasia.

He studied philosophy under Plato, but complained that his master did not give a satisfactory account of the *connection* between the imperishable Forms and their perishable representations, or, as it is put, between " the one and the many." Believing with Plato that eternal Forms existed, he differed, in thinking that those Forms did not exist *apart from their copies*, but rather that they actually dwelt in the perishable bodies of the things to which they gave that Form, and that the conception of their separate existence was nothing but a mental abstraction; to give an instance, manliness was not a something existing apart from men, but was the common nature or Soul that dwelt in all men taken together; men therefore were mixtures of soul and body or mind and matter. But so also had all other species their common nature, Soul or Form, that dwelt in the perishable material bodies of the individuals of each species. The Supreme Mind or God was pure Form without matter, it was complete perfection, separate from the world, and taking no notice of worldly imperfection; but on the other hand, the more or less imperfect Forms of the worldly species were striving to attain the perfection of God, and the desire for that perfection was the source of all motion. A knowledge of this, it was supposed, would enable us to understand what man should do to attain this final end. For that purpose Aristotle tried to establish a science of ethics and with regard to society, a science of politics. Since the more knowledge men possessed, the greater the advantage they would have in striving towards perfection, they should not ignore worldly things altogether, but strive to understand those also; in conformity with the latter teaching he did much work in mapping out the limits of the various sciences, and gave a newer form and content to the general science of logic, the science that underlies all sciences; but he did not, as is popularly supposed, either invent logic, or even give it its name, nevertheless, much of what he did in the domain of logic appears in our text-books to-day, though it required a different economic ground work to show its faults; in those days it must have seemed perfect.

We now go back fifty or sixty years to the definite materialist doctrine of DEMOCRITUS (460—370 B.C., of Abdera in Thrace, on the Ægean Sea), who said there is nothing that is true, or, what is true does not appear to us, for the reason that while sensations are true as far as they go, yet they are only sensations, and consequently cannot constitute the true nature of the objects that cause the sensations. The universe, he thought, consisted of an immense number of material atoms, combined in different ways to produce the different things which he called Forms (of course very different from Plato's), such as sweetness, heat, colour and so on. Each Form gave rise to our sensations by throwing off, as it were, a layer of atoms arranged according to its own peculiar combination, a material image of itself, which image was projected on our organs of sense. This was an early attempt at psychology. The atoms he thought were too small ever to become known by the senses, and could be understood only by the faculty of Reflection; they needed no Creator, for they had always existed, and by their own inherent movements had collided and combined to produce the many different bodies of which our senses are aware. Democritus therefore had no divine principle in his philosophy as had Plato and Aristotle.

It may be convenient at this point to give the gist of the Sceptics' argument. The most notable among them was PYRRHO (date unknown—of Elis), who maintained that the only knowledge we had was that of sensation, but, we could not get at truth through our senses, because we could not say for certain that they represented objects outside us, and since Reason of necessity had only sensations to reason about, then Reason was just as powerless; so no positive statement could be made about anything, for nothing could ever be proved or disproved.

It remains for us to notice two schools, the Epicurean and the Stoic, each a mixture of certain lines of thought already noticed. The Epicurean takes its name from EPICURUS (342—272 B.C., of Samos), whose teaching was a further development of that of the Cyrenaic school of pleasure, though it was not so extreme as has been believed. Their psychology and physics they derived from Democritus, which means they believed in a permanent material world wherein sensation was due to the flow of material atoms. With this, it follows they did not recognise any divine principle, and accordingly quarrelled severely with the Stoics, from whom much of their misrepresentation as being sensualist has come. Since they rejected the divine principle in Platonic and Aristotelian systems their ethics rest upon their own Reason, combined with Free Will. So, the atomic or purely material basis of Democritus was the ground work of their sensations, and agreeable and disagreeable sensations were the bases of moralities, therefore whatever was pleasant became the rightful object of existence.

ZENO (360—270 B.C., of Citium, a small city in Cyprus), the representative stoic, began his philosophical career by joining the Cynics, but their manners were too gross and indecent. He studied in, and learned from, other schools, particularly the Platonic, and finally opened a school of his own in the Stoa, or Porch, from which it got the name of the Stoic. At Zeno's time Greece, honeycombed with sophistry, scepticism, indifference, sensuality and Epicurean softness, was fast going to pieces. Zeno tried to save his people by an appeal to their manliness, and by an attempt to re-establish morality on a basis that would be sound because independent of human frailty.

The Sceptics said that truth could not be attained because sensation, which could not be trusted, was all there was to work with. The Stoics replied that some sensations *must* be true if some are false, for it is impossible to have error without truth, and that Reason distinguishes between them by sifting the clear evidence from the unclear, or that which in reality is not evidence; this amounted to the statement that " evidence needs no proof." In nature they saw two elements, the matter, and God or the Reason which governs matter. They did not believe in free will, but in a destiny arranged by God, who was the only Reason in the world. Their morality was a rigid suppression of sensuous enjoyment, a doctrine fundamentally the same as the Cynics', but purified of much of the grossness. This hardening of the mind and cultivation of fortitude under severe strain, even unto death, were the characteristics which made their teaching acceptable to the conquering Romans, because it had much in common with the latter's own harder nature. Since the Sceptics had reduced knowledge to the limits of sensation, and since the Stoics could not believe this but could find no satisfactory answer, they fell back on faith in that Reason which to them was God directing the world; so we see philosophy as philosophy at the end of its tether for the time being: it sank back into faith, lost its pride and became an aid to religion.

ABSTRACT.—The early philosophers turned away from supernatural myths to the study of nature in the search for essential truth or underlying unity of all things, but not finding this in material objects, turned to the study of Mind and Thinking. They discovered or invented logic, a method of thinking which enabled them to arrange their thoughts and to make distinctions between universals and particulars, the one and the many. But this only increased their difficulties, because it divided the universe into Mind and Matter without in any way explaining the obvious connection between the two, while it destroyed their confidence in finding truth by the aid of sense perception.

The result manifested itself in two main lines of thought, on the one hand Scepticism, wherein nothing could be known, and on the other Morality, the Stoic branch of which relied for its essential truth on faith in the supernatural; the relatively unthinking people simply took life as it came and in the ordinary common-sense manner wandered on from day to day. Therefore philosophy started by throwing faith overboard, only after two and a half centuries to return to it. The positive result achieved was the evolution of their method of enquiry, the logic referred to above; but this did not attain scientific value until it had been considerably modified in much later times, nor was there any real science of thinking until our own times. Meanwhile we must witness the rise of Christianity, and the combination of philosophy and religion.

CHAPTER III

Decadence of Greek Philosophy

We have said that philosophy returned to faith, though if we look closely we shall see that, apart from the Ionian school, some germs of faith had been running through it all the time; nor could it very well have been otherwise, for whenever people take up a new study they cannot help being influenced by their previous thinking, therefore they of necessity approach it with a certain degree of bias. Of course philosophers are just the people who are supposed to have no bias, a mistaken view which was shown very plainly in the Italian school, in the interest they took in individual souls and their transmigration. But taken on the whole, Greek philosophy was fairly free from religious trammels, for there was no powerful priesthood, or sacred book, nor did the philosophers interest themselves overmuch in their popular pagan gods. It is true Anaxagoras had been banished for blaspheming the sun and moon by saying they were made of the same sort of matter as the earth; Socrates had been executed because of his rationalist tendencies, and Aristotle had been indicted for impiety; but in all these cases there were powerful political motives, the religious one being only a cloak. Such conflict as there was between philosophy and religion, particularly in their later developments, arose from the fact that they were both concerned with the same problems, namely, those concerning the nature of that ultimate reality which both have called God. Consequently, given a certain degree of social development, neither could exist without the other, and in this chapter we shall be occupied in tracing the main converging lines of religious and philosophic thought.

Barbarian ignorance of natural phenomena such as thunder, storms, floods, germination, birth (conception), death, etc., was the basis on which arose religious practices and as society developed according to changing economic conditions, there came into being social classes of different grades, one of which was the priestly caste beginning with such rude forms as, for example, the medicine men of the uncivilised American Indians. These men became the doctors and historians of the tribe, and necessarily such learning as there was, apart from technicalities of fishing, hunting, etc., became their particular stock-in-trade. In time they became the especial guardians of all sacred traditions and ritual, and in such a superstitious age were regarded as sacred and holy men, fit to teach and direct the people, for they only were in touch with the gods. Each tribe had its own god, consequently, as their small worlds opened out through trade and conquest, the conflict of different gods ended in the triumph of the idea of there being only one God. But in proportion as this idea gained ground, so did the local character of the tribal god disappear, his place being taken by a God who no longer dwelt in one's own village but away somewhere, always away; he was an unapproachable God except through the medium of the priests and prophets.

In India, out of a personified nature worship arose Vedism, the early faith of Hindu-Aryans, and from this came Brahmanism. Brahma was the Creator, and was a unitarian God. Brahmanism was taught by a priestly caste, but later developed into Hinduism, with a trinity and a splitting up of worship. In Persia, Zoroaster, about 800 B.C., taught one God with a personal divinity; while in Syria the wandering Semitic tribes from the South and East, who became the Jewish nation, and who had the tribal religions of Moses and other prophets, eventually developed the idea of the one God of Israel.

Throughout the growth of the idea of one God, and as the village or tribal god vanished into the misty regions of the sky, the question of *the relation of God to man, and the character of the link or mediator between them necessarily became of more importance.* Here we see our old philosophical friend, the question of the one and the many, mind and matter, God and the world. Since the Jews lived right across the great north road from Egypt to Assyria, with Palestine as their centre, they were open to attack from all sides, and as their tribal gods had vanished and could no longer help them, their prophets foretold that the Great God Jehovah would send a Messiah, who would deliver them from their troubles; then, as we all know, Christ was born, and after a short life claimed to be that very Messiah, the link between heaven and earth. The Christian religion gradually spread along the northern shores of Africa and across the Mediterranean to Italy, ultimately to become, in the form of the Catholic Church, the dominant religion of the Holy Roman Empire.

We must now go back about three centuries and call to mind that after the death of Aristotle, Greece began to fall to pieces. The only philosophy that held the field, apart from Aristotelian Science was Stoicism. As Greece was gradually subdued by the Romans, Greek culture naturally suffered considerably, and many of the philosophers fled across the Mediterranean to Egypt. Their Stoic doctrine was largely Platonic, but later underwent a change, dividing broadly into two main streams, one becoming Christian, the other anti-Christian. The anti-Christian embodied characteristics that differed from those of Plato's time; we therefore distinguish between the old Platonic school and the New Platonists, or Neoplatonists, who took their rise about the time of Christ, and who opposed Christianity. Just as the meeting of Ionian and Italian philosophers in Athens produced dialectics, and ultimately the science of logic, so did the meeting of Stoic philosophers, or their disciples, with the early Christians, lead to Christian Theology; though we have here to do not so much with Greeks, as with men of other nationalities who had been influenced by Greek culture.

Since our work in the main is to follow philosophy, evidently it is not our business to discuss theology except in so far as its development takes into account questions of a philosphical character, such as the freedom of the will, the relation between men and God, or between the many and the one. In doing this we must bear in mind that philosophy had developed two broad lines; first, Scepticism, which of course had nothing to do with religion, because it did not accept anything as being known to be true; and second, Morality, which was represented by Epicureans on the one hand and Stoics on the other. Epicureans, as we have seen, did not believe in any divine principle, while the Stoics did, as of course did Christians. Epicureanism entailed the belief in a free will, which was in accord with Christianity, though its belief in atomism with no divine principle was the very reverse. It was therefore the Stoics who were the most philosophically inclined to accept Christian principles. But the Stoics pinned their faith to " destiny," and accordingly did not believe in the freedom of the will, and unless this principle is accepted the Christian doctrine of atonement is useless, for if responsibility for one's acts is not recognised and accepted, atonement for sin has no meaning. Therefore those of the Stoics and others who refused to come to terms with Christianity, developed a religious belief of a mystical character; these were the Neoplatonists; we will return to them later.

The question of free will, which, by the way, " philosophers " have not yet settled, led to a discussion which ended in the general acceptance of the Christian position (though even in the Church there was much disagreement, as, for example, between Augustine and Pelagius in the beginning of the fifth century), which is that God is the source of all that is good, that man has a free will to chose either good or evil, but when he choses to do what he knows to be right, at that moment God gives him the Grace to carry out his intention. It was therefore not in his own strength that a Christian fulfilled the moral law, but by the Grace of God. To win this Grace one must have faith in God and be a member of God's Holy (wholly or one) Church. The Christian counted himself a child of God by right of initiation through baptism, which could apply to all men willing to become members of the one Holy Church, whereas the Jew was a child of God only by right of nationality, and the Stoic by individual right. Therefore the possibility of applying the Christian principle of initiation to all mankind, along with the feeling we all have of acting freely, and the feeling that we must take the consequences of our acts, won recognition in Roman times, the more so because it was allied with the hardness of the Stoic temper, though not in such an extreme form as early Stoicism.

From the philosophic standpoint, however, it was more particularly the principle of having a mediator between the one and the many that formed the link between Platonic philosophy and Christian faith, and this mediator was Jesus Christ, who was at one and the same time both God and man, and was, moreover, the only mediator.

There were other partially christianised systems of religion that, largely influenced by their many former and not entirely disregarded pagan gods, indulged their fancy with long chains of mediators or divine beings of different grades, and this tendency reacted on Christianity in the institution of saints and angels; though these have never by the authorities of the Church been identified with the Divine nature, for Christ alone was both God and man.

We have seen that Christians believed first, that God was One; second, that His character was exemplified in the life of Christ; and third, that personal intercourse with God or Jesus was to be attained by loving service to other men, for " Inasmuch as ye have done it unto one of the least of these my brethren, ye have done it unto me" (Matt. xxv., 40). This kind of religious belief gave rise to the philosophical question, what is there in the nature of God and of man and of the mediator between them which allows of such intercourse, or, what is the unity amidst all this multiplicity.

or, to put it another way, how can God the Father, God the Son, and the universal Spirit that dwells in the faithful, or God the Holy Ghost, be three (a Trinity) and at the same time one (a Unity)? The view taken by Christian theologians is that these three distinct elements, each of which is God, find their unity *in Love,* wherein all believers, even the most lowly, may be united with God the Father through Jesus Christ, who establishes the connection of the Supreme Godhead with the material world. So we see that one branch of Stoic philosophy became absorbed by, and subordinated to, Christian Theology, and as far as Europe was concerned remained in that humble position throughout the Middle Ages.

Let us now go back to the other branch of the Stoics and those who still thought after the manner of the older schools, who became anti-Christian—the Neoplatonists. Here again we see a conflux of two streams, but this time it is between Platonic philosophy and eastern religious thought of the theosophical brand which came from farther East than the seat of Christianity. The Neoplatonists, in working out the idea of mediation, sought rather to keep the Godhead separate from the material world, while Christians had sought to definitely connect them in the person of Jesus Christ. Christians brought God down into the world, Neoplatonists made the world strive towards God.

Philosophy, we remember, had been exiled from Greece. In its old home Scepticism had killed it. " It had started with the doubt of the child, had asked its questions, attempted answers, and had finished with the doubt of old age;" all it had left behind of permanent value was a partly developed method of thinking—Aristotelian logic. But if it found no worshippers in Greece, it was welcomed in Egypt, where the doctrines were new and therefore interesting. In Alexandria several schools were formed, and here took place the early struggles between Neoplatonist and Christian. This city, lying in the track of a later sea trading route between East and West, was naturally a great centre of commerce, and in science came to rival Athens. All those people who sought a refuge from Scepticism, together might be called the Alexandrian school, while the Neoplatonists constituted the most illustrious section of that movement; in following them we shall see the final act in the drama of Greek Philosophy.

Greek ideas of course had taken root in Alexandria long before Christ, but Neoplatonism proper began with a Jew named PHILO (born c. 20 B.C., of Alexandria), who represented a mixture of Greek dialectics and Eastern mysticism. He had learned dialectics from the works of Plato and others, but the New Academicians (almost complete sceptics, who taught long after Plato in Plato's old school, the Academy), Arcesilaus and Carneades, had taught him to apply the method sceptically. In the spirit of these men he distrusted all knowledge gained by the senses, and since Reason, reasoned on the basis of such knowledge, then Reason itself could not get at truth. But besides Greek dialectics of that kind he possessed a large measure of Oriental mysticism, which led him to say that though the Senses and Reason were powerless, and thus far he was a philosopher, there was still the faculty of Faith, and this, the gift of God, was real Science or Knowledge; his philosophy then became theology. With Philo, God was the one Unity; his nature could never be known, but we knew of his existence in the " The Word." This " Word " had a twofold character, it was first, God's thought (mind), and second, God's thought carried out or expressed in the existing world as we know it (matter). We have already seen the subordination of one branch of philosophy to Christianity; we now see the other trying to establish a rival theology and to found a Church. As regards Epicureanism, this had long ago become indifferent, a sort of common-sense scepticism.

Following Philo came PLOTINUS (c. 203—262 A.D., an Egyptian), the greatest of the Neoplatonists, who thought with Plato that nothing but universals (Forms) could be true (see Fig. I). We knew phenomena through our senses, and the universals we knew through our intelligence acting in relation to sense perceptions, but, since that ended the reasoning process, how were we to know God? Plotinus answered, that since Reason could go no farther, we could only know God when in a state of ecstacy, wherein Reason plays no part, for Reason, if it could know the infinite would have to *be* the Infinite; therefore we could only know God by *being* God, and in a state of ecstacy or rapture we became part of, or rather absorbed in God, and only in this way could we come to know God. God stood revealed to us only because we had become One with Him. This state of rapture, he thought, might be gained in some natures by Music (including poetry, beauty, rythm and such like); other natures, such as those of philosophers, were ravished through the contemplation of Unity and Proportion (the wonderful order in the universe); others again, by the pursuit of moral perfection executed in the sphere of love and prayer. Ecstacy was not the connection between the one and the many, the passage from one state to the other was made without such a mundane and even vulgar nuisance as a connection, for such would have defiled the pure essence of God.

The Alexandrian Trinity (some say the Christian idea of the Trinity was an imitation of the Alexandrian, others say the reverse) consisted of three persons; the third, or most inferior grade, was the soul or cause of all the activity and life in worldly things; the second was the Intelligence or universal Being (universals); the first was not Being of any kind, but simply Unity. Since Unity was not Being, it was something that could never be conceived in thought; it was not nothing, but "*that which* thought, *that which* existed." In like manner the circus clown says the world rests on a rock, and that on another rock, and that on the bottom; but this bottom is unexplainable, mysterious; and the Alexandrian Unity had the same mysterious character. So we see that what remained of Platonic philosophy lost itself in mysticism—the mysticism of the supernatural. (Let the reader reserve his laugh until he has "done his bit" to free the modern world from the same sort of thing; for there are plenty of mystics living to-day whose breasts swell with ecstatic fervour while they listen to sermons, march to "glory," or, drunk with breath-arresting asthetics, pay court in a hundred other ways to "the beautiful.")

With regard to the creation of the world, Christians said that God created it out of nothing, for, being all powerful, one thing was as easy as another. The Alexandrian dialecticians maintained that out of nothing nothing could come; they therefore accounted for the world of many things by saying the many were simply emanations of God's *will*, that is, the many consisted of God's *acts*, not his substance.

From Alexandria, Plotinus went to Rome, and was there associated with Porphyry and Iamblicus. In Rome the Alexandrian school became a sort of Church, and disputed with Christianity for world empire. Christianity ascended the throne in the person of Constantine. Afterwards Neoplatonism was represented there by Julian; but Christianity did not depend upon support from Emperors, and continued to flourish after it lost Constantine, whereas when the Neoplatonists lost Julian they lost power and influence. Their last fight for philosophic life took place with PROCLUS (412—485 A.D., of Xanthus, Asia Minor, afterwards Alexandria and Athens) as leader. He took Plato as an idol. The inscription, "Know thyself," on the temple at Delphi, Socrates had taken as an exhortation to ethical study. Plato had taken it to mean that in knowing one's self, that is, in knowing one's mind, one would become acquainted with the eternal Forms. But Proclus thought that in knowing ourselves we really know the divine One, of whom oneself is but a ray of that Unity. With Proclus metaphysics is the only possible science; it descends to us from above, and is more perfect than that which is the result of investigation. "Invention is the energy of the soul." "Omnes Scientia vera est a Deo" (All true knowledge comes from God).

Proclus, the last genius of Neoplatonism, had tried to give it new life, but had failed, and under Justinian the Alexandrian school became extinct. With this we may say that Greek philosophy came to an end in its original home, for with the sack of Rome in the fifth century, by barbarians from the North, and the general subjugation of the Pagan civilisations of southern Europe, learning in these regions suffered shipwreck; libraries were destroyed, and the main portion of Aristotelian philosophy and science migrated mainly to Syria, Arabia and Persia. Meanwhile in Europe, as already stated, a modified Platonic philosophy became the handmaid of Roman Catholicism, and continued in that character through the Dark Ages.

ABSTRACT.—With the Stoics, philosophy returned to faith. One portion of it became a sort of works manager to Christian Faith, while the other trickled out in mysticism. The only positive result was the evolution of a partial method of logical thinking that required further perfecting; in this lay the progress. Apart somewhat from the above we have seen the bases of two great lines of what became traditional thought— the Pagan and the Christian. The Pagan thinking, symbolised under the name of Aristotelianism, included the physical science of the times, while Christian thought appeared as the teaching of the Roman Catholic Church.

CHAPTER IV

Philosophy in the Middle Ages

As the destruction of the Roman Empire had made learning and the pursuit of knowledge on the former scale impossible, through libraries being scattered, endowments of centres of learning being confiscated, and so on; teachers and scholars not under the auspices of the Church had to seek a living elsewhere. They went to Asia, whilst Christian theologians and teachers remained in Europe. We shall now follow those two branches of thought to show how they ultimately unite in the twelfth and thirteenth centuries, and also the consequent conflict of their separate influences during the Renaissance.

The philosophy of Christianity was mainly Platonic, but the Church possessed a little Aristotelian influence, principally in the domain of science, more particularly in the science of logic. When the shipwreck of learning took place, by far the greater portion of Aristotle's works were lost, or rather lost to Europe; but one of the barbarian chieftains, Theodoric, himself not a scholar, appointed as his ministers Cassiodorus and Boethius, two of the most learned men at his disposal, who were to save what they could from the wreck. Cassiodorus (born about 480) founded monasteries, wherein monks were to preserve such books as they had, and were to study them. This had a great influence in determining the available order and extent of study throughout the Middle Ages, because it brought about the fact that during that period learning was under the control of the faithful, which meant under the control of the Catholic Church. Boethius (c. 470—524) occupied himself very largely in translating from Greek to Latin works of Plato, Aristotle, Euclid, Archimedes and Porphyry. Porphyry, we remember, was the friend of Plotinus, a Neoplatonist and opponent of Christianity, but he had written an introduction to Aristotle's logic. This book, being only an introduction, was necessarily very elementary, but of logic they had very little else from the ninth to the twelfth century. Logic is concerned with making distinctions between different things, or between different parts of a thing, that they may be better understood through the different things or parts being arranged or classified. Porphyry's book dealt with minor and relatively unimportant distinctions between Genera, Species, Differences, Properties and Accidents; these were known as the five predicables, and were supposed to represent the different classes or grades of qualities possessed by things; for example, taking the word "animal" as the Genus, this Genus includes many Species of animals, such as fish, the horse or man. But man possesses many qualities called Differences, by which he differs from all other species, such as the power of articulate speech. He also possesses other qualities called Properties, not so sharply defined as differences, but yet possessed by the whole species, for instance, a relative capacity for argument. And finally, by accident as it were, men may or may not be tall, ugly, fair or thickskinned, etc.; such qualities, which do not apply to the whole class are termed Accidents. Porphyry's elementary logic, although it called attention to the relation between Genera and Species, yet did not attempt the solution, for that question was too big for such a small work, being in fact the root question in philosophy—the one and the many, mind and matter, God and the world, the Trinity, etc.; nor did it receive any particular attention throughout the Dark Ages, a period consisting of from four to five centuries, during which no great thinkers came to light; but it became the central point of discussion during the Scholastic period, which occupied from about the ninth to the fifteenth century, for in the ninth century an intellectual ferment began, which developed in itensity as time went on.

The scholars of those times, or the Schoolmen as they are called, had received their training in the form of Christian tradition, and to question the roots of that teaching was no light task, the more so since they themselves were men of faith. Nevertheless, they began to ask awkward questions concerning Genera and Species, and even attempted answers. This gave rise to a discussion between what were called the Nominalists and the Realists. ANSELM (1033—1109, Archbishop of Canterbury from 1093 till his death), whose doctrine came ultimately from Plato, was a realist who believed that universals (see Fig. 1) had a real existence; ROSCELLINUS, his contemporary, took (partly from Aristotle) the opposite view, that only individuals (the so-called copies of the universals) really existed, and that universals were no more than names, that is, that they existed only nominally. The latter view, of course, denies the Oneness of the three Gods—the doctrine of the Trinity. The discussion lasted for centuries; meanwhile the scholastics practised the art of argument and sharpened their wits by means of elementary logic to such an extent that many of them, such as Roscellinus and PETER ABELARD (1079—1142, of Palais, near Nantes, later a theologian of Notre Dame, Paris) were becoming heretics. They were substituting reason for faith, and that could not be tolerated by the Fathers of the Church at any cost. The whole period was one of confused thinking and hair splitting arguments, so much so that the Schoolmen, with their characteristic doubt, resembled the Sophists of Socrates' time. There was accordingly a philosophical disruption taking place, which might (so it appears on the surface) possibly have been kept under by the rulers of the Church, had it not been that in the twelfth century many of the lost works of Aristotle at last made their way into Europe. This recovery led to important philosophical developments, and as a prelude to a discussion of these we now go back to the dispersal of those works to briefly follow their course from Greece to Asia and back to Europe.

The last of the Greek philosophers had been driven by Justinian (483—565, Emperor of Constantinople and Rome) to find refuge in Asia, and were welcomed in Persia, but particularly in Bagdad. They took with them the works of Aristotle, and the philosophy contained in them became the basis of that which is called Arabian. It is not Arabian, however, but Greek, Jewish and Persian. Arabian philosophy represented a small section of a great Mohammedan movement, and at bottom constituted a reaction against Islam. Islamism is a wide-spread religion founded by Mahomet (or Mohammed, 571—632), who imagined himself the apostle of God; its centre was Mecca, in Arabia. After the death of Mahomet it spread north-east to Samarkand and Bokhara (North of Afghanistan), north to Armenia and Turkey, and north-west along the northern shores of Africa to Morocco, and to Cordova in Andalusia (southern Spain). The reaction to which we have referred arose in those distant parts of the Arabian Empire.

The Arabs were illiterate, but as they spread, they endeavoured to glorify their dynasty with Letters, and found many Greeks, Jews and Christians willing to give them Arabian and Syriac translations of Athenian and Alexandrian writers. Thus it came about that Aristotle was presented under the guise of Arabian philosophy, and was also mixed up with Alexandrian science. Europe then is indebted to the Arabs for the preservation of those Greek writings that had such an influence during the period immediately preceding the Renaissance.

While learning in Christian Europe in the tenth century was decadent, Andalusia under Mohammedan rule was the centre of light, and from Cordova, the above mentioned city, came Averroes (c. 1126—1198). who was born there. He translated, and commented on, Aristotle's teaching, and his writings constituted one of the principal media by which Arab culture spread slowly through Europe. We have already seen that disputes were going on in Parisian theological quarters, and that the Church of Rome had found it difficult to keep heresy in check; but when the later works of Aristotle were introduced, which seemed to offer an explanation of almost everything, the disputes were furious and deep. Aristotle had taught that the world was eternal, had not been created, and would not end; he had also taught that individual souls (though not the soul of the species) were mortal, thus denying the Christian doctrine of immortality; in fact this question of what constituted an individual as distinct from a universal was always obtruding. These doctrines were, moreover, supported by a more advanced logic than had been at the disposal of the men of Abelard's time. They were, of course, directly opposed to Christian teaching, so, to get such questions settled became a very urgent matter. THOMAS AQUINAS (1226—1274, of Aquino, Italy), a Dominican, took the affair in hand and tried to reconcile Aristotle and the Church. By his working out he arrived at the idea that certain truths might be discovered by man's reason, but there were other truths that could only be known through supernatural revelation, "though he loved Aristotle, he loved the Church more." This ending to the attempt to reconcile the two great lines of traditional thought—the Pagan and the Christian, or logic (reason) and faith, only meant that what could not be logically explained by reason *in such a manner that it would satisfy faith*, must be left to faith. However, there were other thinkers who were not satisfied, because both traditions were dogmatic, both had been regarded as infallible, and both were concerned with the question of essential truth, yet embodied different and apparently irreconcilable conclusions, so what could be made of it all? DUNS SCOTUS (c. 1274—1308, British), a Franciscan, tried to reconcile Nominalism and Realism, even as Aquinas had tried, though he quarrelled with the latter on some points, being more inclined to give prominence to the reality of the individual, in so far as he thought that the individual nature was a higher perfection of the universal nature; in other words, he had a strong leaning towards Nominalism. WILLIAM of OCCAM (died 1350, of Ockham, in Surrey), another Franciscan, went much farther towards Nominalism, the growth of which, since it cut out the reality of universals, represented a desire to escape from both Christian and Classical tradition. On the other hand, WILLIAM of CHAMPEAUX was an out and out realist. There were indeed some who thought of a double standard of truth —that a thing might be true in philosophy but not in theology, and *vice versa,* however, this need not be discussed, as it was evidently quite unsatisfactory and left no particular historic mark. It should go without saying that Faith neither had or has any need to reason or to argue, and we can see clearly how in doing so it began its own undoing, for the fight between Reason and Faith led to greater freedom in thinking, and, taken on the whole, it became impossible any longer to reconcile philosophy and theology; but to understand the utter confusion of thought prevailing with gradually increasing intensity throughout the Scholastic period, and which culminated in the breakdown of both Classical and Christian tradition, we shall have to look at the material development underlying it.

In pre-Christian and early Christian times Greece and Rome were founded on wealth produced by chattel slaves. In its early days Christianity had a hard fight, but had become well established by the fifth century, at which period pagan Rome became subject to northern invaders. The object of conquest was, of course, that the conquered might pay tribute, but tribute involved the labour of the slaves, therefore extermination would not have served the purpose of the conquerors; instead, many of the new rulers or kings became converted to Christianity, and so ruled their subjects through concessions to the Pope, who held Spiritual Power over the mass of the people; many even received their coronation at his hands in spiritual righteousness. But the kings did not forget to fight among themselves for the purpose of extending their domains and acquiring wealth and power. For this purpose, as time went on, they required ever greater and greater numbers of fighting men and trusted leaders. The leaders received in payment grants of land, subject to a promise to fight for the kings when necessary. But land without labour was no use, and as the land was granted on conditions of armed service on the kings' behalf, so also was the labour that worked the land. And so it came about that where former masters actually owned slaves in the way they owned cattle, afterwards the slaves were not owned in person, but were attached to the land, and should a lord be deposed in favour of another, the slaves or serfs stayed where they were under the new master. Since the system of landholding was founded on military service, or fighting, it is spoken of as Feudalism. There existed, then, a Spiritual Power and a Military Power, both of which required monetary support. The Church claimed tithes (the tenth part of a man's income) for its clergy, who had to remit a portion to Rome. Evidently what found its way to Rome could not go into the pockets of the kings, and naturally Church and kings quarrelled about "their rights," the Church enforcing its views by threats of excommunication; and excommunication was never a small affair to a good Catholic, for " what doth it profit a man if he gain the whole world and suffer the loss of his own soul? "

Occasionally Rome claimed extraordinary tributes, and for both ordinary and extraordinary, employed Italian merchants to collect the dues in the form of merchandise, mainly wool, to have it dyed and woven, to sell it and forward the proceeds, less a commission, to Rome. These merchants became the Florentine bankers. At the same time, there were many wandering Jewish merchants and traders also amassing money, with which they could accommodate needy kings and nobles. Incidentally, we might point to the cultural influence of these traders, who knew the different languages of the people with whom they did business, and who were therefore a great factor in the spread of learning in art, in literature, in science, in law, in comparative religion, in the keeping of accounts, and, therefore, in stewardship and the management of estates, etc. As a blow against the rising power of money, the Church condemned usury, so in virtue of that condemnation, the nobles could satisfy at one and the same time both their spiritual conscience and their material well being, by refusing to pay interest on borrowed money. Therefore, while the nobility quarrelled with the Church, both were interested in opposing the monetary power *as power in the hands of the trading or merchant class,* while requiring it as power for themselves.

Students of economic history are well aware that the rise of the merchant class was the result of *continued improvement in tools and general modes of producing wealth, which caused a greater and greater output; requiring extensive travel to secure markets and materials; all tending to the formation of different groups, with different interests, which reflected themselves in correspondingly different modes of thought expressed in the form of different political interests.* Politically, England, France, Holland, and Spain became nations with national interests opposed to each other, and to the restraints of the international Church, while within those nations were groups with particular interests opposed to the Church on the one hand and the kings and nobles on the other. These groups were the merchants, who required workers freed from the feudal nobility, that is, freed from the land so that they might be freely exploited through working for wages; they wanted also to be free from the necessity of paying tribute to Rome, and from many of the ordinances emanating from there. They rebelled against the laws of kings and the laws of the Church, and at the end of the fifteenth century they had reached the stage at which they were willing to pay the price of excommunication from the Catholic Church, because by that time their philosophical representatives had discovered a new way to heaven *via* the Reformation.

It may help us to understand the confusion that prevailed in philosophy during the scholastic period if we remember that for some centuries certain nobles could attain more power and influence by supporting the king, others by supporting the Church, mainly indirectly through supporting some other king, while the trading class had been gradually rising; and that the sons of these people, or poor students for whom they found money, had gone to the schools and carried with them the mental reflection of the material interests of whichever class or group they represented. The new theological and anti-theological mentality of the opponents of the Church, apparently unconnected with material interests, was simply the indirect rationalisation of those interests, and was accordingly governed by the general material conditions of the period. Viewed in this light, the philosophic confusion appears to be merely the abstract general reflex of the material or economic confusion between the older and the newer tools or modes of wealth production, which produced the merchants, the breakdown of manorial economy, and the rise of the monetary system, and which brought in its train new social relations requiring correspondingly new ideas of justice and right. We may also add to these the individual or personal desires of the disputants, an example of which may be found in Martin Luther (1483—1546), whose famous doctrine, " man is justified by faith alone," typified the desire to please oneself about ordinances, penances, celibacy, etc. All those things together formed the groundwork of the Reformation, for in order to do what they felt they must, if their interests were to be served, and which, therefore, *seemed to them to be right*, it was necessary to attack what, to them, was an intolerable religious authority; but, being godly men, they were not prepared to overthrow religion altogether, so what else could they do but find fault with the existing religious doctrine and reform it? The Reformation was merely the outward result of their spiritual justification for doing what economic forces had driven them to do. It marked the downfall of Papal supremacy in many European countries. Christian tradition had received a blow from which it never recovered, and in consequence Philosophy had much more freedom, not because the new churches were more tolerant, but because the weight of ancient authority was gone. From that time to the present Christianity has split itself into an ever-increasing mass of contending ruins—the *débris* of a faded mentality. The Catholic Church does, indeed, maintain consistency amid its absurdity, but the rest are absurd without even being consistent.

Now how was it with the other tradition—that of Aristotle? In 1453, a century before the death of Luther, the Turks captured Constantinople; this made an end of the Holy Roman Empire, but it also caused Greek scholars to flee into Italy, and thus brought the Greek versions of Aristotle within reach of French and German students. They had now no need to rely on Arabian and Latin translations, the works of Plato and Aristotle could be read in the original, and so was classical antiquity seen more clearly. Aristotle had taught that the sun moved round the earth, and that it was made of a material different from that of the earth; that the earth was still and flat; also several other doctrines which, to the men of the late fifteenth and the early sixteenth centuries, seemed equally absurd. But why had these doctrines become absurd? To see this we must glance at the scientific attainments of the age.

In the Middle Ages the investigation of natural phenomena had been neglected. There had, indeed, been a few alchemists who aimed at making base metals into gold, but in the thirteenth century the beginnings of positive science may be seen in the ideas of Albertus Magnus (1193—1280), a Dominican, and ROGER BACON (1214—1294), a Franciscan. Roger Bacon, a monk of Oxford, thought that Aristotle's logic, which took some statement as being true and then made deductions from it, was insufficient unless the statement or premise from which the deductions were made had first been established by the inductive method of observation and experiment. This amounts to saying that deduction is all right in its place, but its place is *after* its premises have been established by reason first examining natural phenomena, observing what takes place, and then experimenting to verify the result, that is, to see if the same result will always follow from the same material combinations. This method of searching for truth is not based on reason only, but rather is reason itself based upon actual experiment with natural phenomena; it attacked religion because it put experiment before *authority*, and it attacked philosophy because it put experiment before *logic,* so where previously there had been a split between Theology (faith) and Philosophy (reason or logic), there now came a split between Philosophy and Science (experiment and verification) concerning the proper method to use in searching for truth. Roger Bacon and "the Blessed Albert," through their knowledge of nature, were regarded as conjurors in the popular mind, but as dangerous thinkers by their theological superiors. The inductive method was employed with wider scope three centuries after R. Bacon by FRANCIS BACON (1561—1626, of London, for a time Lord Chancellor), who is known as the father of English materialism, though it must be remembered that these early materialists were not so complete as they have been represented, their idea was that by employing the inductive method of research they might gain a better and more complete knowledge of God's purposes through understanding God's works in nature. Bacon's method of starting from experienced facts, both positive and negative, was not followed entirely by succeeding students, nevertheless, it has had a powerful influence; nor did he succeed in giving to the world a complete philosophy of the whole range of natural phenomena, attempted in later days by COMTE (1798—1857, of Montpellier, later Paris), and still later by HERBERT SPENCER (1820—1903, of Derby); we shall see the reason in Part II. So much for the method of science, now—a few facts. At the end of the fifteenth century Copernicus, a Polish mathematician, had taught, with great success, the older idea that not the earth but the sun was the centre of our planetary system, and that the earth was round and continually moving, thus giving the lie to Aristotle. Columbus had taken the rotundity as a fact in an endeavour to avoid Arab plunderers on the route to India, and had discovered America in 1492. Vesalius, at no great distance in the sixteenth century, had laid the basis of modern anatomy, which again gave the lie to Aristotelian speculations. William Gilbert, a little later, founded the science of terrestrial magnetism, which explained much that had hitherto been mysterious. Hans Lippershey, in 1608, invented the telescope, which was perfected by Galileo, who succeeded, by means of it, in spoiling quite a number of ancient astronomical ideas; he also discovered the isochronism of the pendulum, and the laws of falling bodies, proving the previous reasoning on those points to be definitely wrong. Kepler, about the end of the sixteenth century, formulated the laws of motion. Under the weight of all this, what could happen to Aristotelian tradition but that it should fall into the dust of a memory? If we ask why it was that Aristotle should have made such serious mistakes, we may answer in a sentence, that in Aristotle's time the tools had not been in existence, which alone could bring about the newer understanding.

We are now in a position to see how material development undermined both Christian and Pagan traditions. Philosophy had split into science on the one hand, and a philosophy that was independent of theology on the other; it left the supreme mind of God to theology, and proceeded to an examination of the human mind. Theology began to crack up in the interests of a multiplication of religious forms, but its exponents did not give up without a fight, they developed very vicious tendencies before settling down to emulate the Lamb of God. This latter may be seen in the incident of Giordano Bruno, who, on the strength of the Copernican theory of the sun being the centre of our planetary system, had become a heresiarch by saying that certain statements in the Bible were wrong. For this the Inquisition, in 1600, had him tied to a stake in Rome and publicly burnt alive. And we may also, perhaps, be in a better position for understanding that much quoted, but little understood, passage by **Karl**

Marx—" In every historical epoch, the prevailing mode of economic production and exchange, and the social organisation necessary following from it, form the basis upon which is built up, and from which alone can be explained, the political and intellectual history of that epoch."

ABSTRACT FROM THE BEGINNING.—In the first chapter we saw that animal evolution resulted in the development or organs of sense, nerves and brains, and that social evolution gave rise to an interpretation of the mysterious, expressed in religious practices and mythology founded on faith. In the second, that Greek philosophers threw over tale-telling, studied nature, developed philosophy, dialectics, logic and material science; that logic led to scepticism, the decadence of philosophy and a return to faith. In the third, that one line of philosophy became extinct in ecstatic mysticism, while the other became the servant of Christianity, the remainder of Pagan culture coming through mainly in the form of Aristotelian science. And in the present chapter we get the two long lines of Pagan and Christian tradition where, in the twelfth century conflict of the two, Pagan logic does much to smash Christian tradition, science helps to perform the same operation on Pagan tradition, while underneath all are the material developments that prepare the ground and ultimately give rise to the modern scientific method of enquiry which produces verifiable results, thereby knocking both traditions to pieces. The Church and the Bible had been infallible, but were found to be not so. Aristotle had been infallible, but the new scientific method of enquiry, plus the new tools and instruments, had shown that not only was the intellectual world moving, but also the very ground under their feet, while the sun that moved daily across the sky was all the time standing still. Old methods of wealth production, with their attendant old philosophical speculations and old religions, all had gone to pieces, their places being taken by new methods and tools, reflected in new conceptions of literature, art, science, religion, law and philosophy; it was the period of re-birth—the Renaissance.

Was it any wonder that the Frenchman, René Descartes, should decide never to believe anything again until he had first tested it by the utmost doubt at his command?

CHAPTER V

Philosophy from Descartes to Kant

In passing to modern philosophy, which began in the seventeenth century, it is important to remember that its exponents were not only mathematicians, but were also much influenced by the results of positive science, though they did not, nor do their followers to-day, apply the scientific method in their philosophical speculations. So once more do we see that the tools and instruments by which the scientific results are attained have an indirect expression in philosophical thinking.

Seventeenth century philosophy may be said to have begun on the materialist side with Francis Bacon, and on the idealist side with DESCARTES (1596—1650, of La Haye, in Touraine, later Paris; in Latin called Cartesius), who cast all notions of ancient philosophy on the scrap heap in order to make a new start; though neither Bacon or Descartes were purely materialist or purely idealist. Descartes began his enquiry by systematically doubting everything, with, however, one exception, for he found he could not doubt that he was thinking. In the very act of thinking of himself as a thinking being, he connected thinking, with himself as the thinker, and realised that as a thinker he was far from being perfect; but since he could not imagine his imperfect self except by comparing it with something perfect (for the *im*perfect could only be conceived as being a lower degree of, or a declination from the idea of complete perfection), he concluded that complete perfection must exist somewhere. In the same way he found from the fact that he himself was finite, that there must be infinity; and again, since a perfect being that did not exist, except in thought, would be a contradiction, for the reason that if it lacked reality it would be imperfect, that being must be *real;* from all of which he deduced *the existence of a real and infinitely perfect being* or God (though not in the Christian sense). This is known as the " ontological argument " for the existence of God, and had been presented about five and a half centuries before by Anselm, without, however, attracting attention, because the Schoolmen had never doubted the existence of something. This real and infinitely perfect being, Descartes thought, if perfect must be truthful, and since perfection in the highest degree must be the source of all the lower degrees it followed that man's ideas about the world, *if true,* were derived from God.

At this point we might mention that Plato had used the word " Idea " to indicate a thing that really existed as an eternal and permanent nature, whether we thought of it or not, and that later, Augustine had taught that such eternal natures might be regarded as thoughts in the mind of God; but by the sixteenth century the latter notion had been extended to mean thoughts in the human mind also; accordingly we now use the word " idea " to mean a thought in the human mind.

Now how did Descartes distinguish between true and false ideas? Here again his Ontology served him, because, he argued, if God is perfect and truthful, and if man's knowledge of the world is got from his knowledge of God, then his knowledge of the world must also be true, and the world *must be a real world provided such knowledge is clear and distinct,* that is, not mixed up with doubtful speculations, for God, being truth, could not deceive him in any way. Clear and distinct notions were accordingly true but, which were they? With Descartes they were those of mathematics and mechanics, or extension and motion. For example, we cannot conceive of a body without some kind of shape that occupies space, or is *extended* in space. And since all bodies occupying space are capable of being separated into parts, modified or re-joined in various ways, all taking place through motion, and as mathematical and mechanical notions are the same wherever we meet them, they are the only clear and distinct notions, for all other ideas, such as colour, warmth, etc., are perceived differently by different people. In this way the decks were cleared for a mechanical conception of the physical universe. THOMAS HOBBES (1588—1679, of Malmesbury, Wiltshire; later Oxford and Paris), who was in touch with Descartes, even thought that consciousness was a kind of motion, but Descartes held the idea that consciousness had no shape, did not occupy space and could not be conceived of as being mathematical; therefore, not being a body, it could not have motion or have anything to do with motion in the physical sense. Accordingly he spoke of bodies or *matter*, and consciousness or *mind*, as being substances exactly opposite to each other, for we could only conceive of them as each being different and independent of the other. Mind and matter, between which lies the greatest distinction in all philosophy, were therefore by him considered to be separate, and this, of course, raised once more the eternal question of the *connection* between the two. How, for example, could the mind by thinking of a certain action make the material body perform that action as, when asking a friend at table to pass the salt, he does so? In dealing with the latter problem Descartes, following mechanical principles, supposed that the heart distilled from the finest particles of the blood, a very fine fluid which was driven to the pineal gland in the brain and there converted by that gland into nervous energy, which passed along the nerves to the muscles, thereby giving rise to motion; and as regards the *connection* between mind and matter, he supposed that the soul or mind of man directed that motion, though it did not produce it. This, it will be seen, did not explain how the direction took place, therefore his explanation was no explanation at all, and the problem remained unsolved.

The theory of Occasionalism taught by some Cartesians (followers of Descartes) was that *no inter-*

action ever took place, but both mind and matter were actuated separately by God, and that on the *occasion* of a man thinking to move his arm God caused the arm to move. In short, that God caused parallel actions of mind and matter.

NICOLE MALEBRANCHE (1638—1715, of Paris) held the idea that there were not three terms—God, mind and matter, but only two—God (the only mind) and matter (the world); and that when human beings formed clear and distinct mental pictures of the world around them, those thoughts were really parts of God's thinking.

SPINOZA (1632—1677, of Amsterdam), a Jew, began as a Cartesian, with accepting the separation of mind and matter, but, through working at the problem of their interdependence, afterwards developed the Pantheistic view. With him there was but one substance in the universe, and that was God. What we called " matter " was one part of God, and what we called " mind " was the other part, or, in other words, mind and matter were but two attributes of God. This concept was a philosophical reflex of the times in which mathematicians and physicists were establishing the universal laws of motion and gravity as being common to all things, regardless of species or particular individuals, whether animals, men or machines. Now the root question in philosophy is that of the unity among individuals—how can *many* individuals be at the same time *one?* Spinoza certainly made an attempt at unity by making all three (God, matter and mind) into one, but he only did so at the expense of the other end of the question, that is, by destroying the idea of individuality. It also destroyed the freedom of the will and all Christian and Jewish notions of God; for the latter he was excommunicated from the Jewish fraternity.

However, LEIBNITZ (1646—1716, of Leipzig) returned to the problem of individuality, and asked, once more, what is an individual? He held that an individual must be a unit in itself, that is, not capable of being divided into parts; but as every particle of matter could be so divided to infinity, real "unities" or "monads," as he called them, could never be found in material bodies, but only in souls, which have no parts. He further imagined that parts of the universe, other than man, might have souls, though of a lower order than that of man, and only to that extent could material things have reality. Such unities, or monads, were the only things that really existed, all else was illusion; they existed as individuals apart from each other; the apparent intercommunication between them was not really such, it resembled Occasionalism, and consisted of a "pre-established harmony" arranged by God, who is the "final cause" of all.

So it would appear that from Descartes' time, mind and matter gradually got more clearly separated, and the problem of truth gradually became the problem of how do human beings perform their thinking? Towards the solution of the latter question, JOHN LOCKE (1632—1704, of Wrington, Somersetshire, later Oxford and London), in 1690, contributed an "Essay concerning Human Understanding." He agreed with Descartes that matter and mind owe their being to God, for the simple reason that something cannot come from nothing, and, therefore, something there must always have been that possessed "power" and "knowledge." But he differed from Descartes in that he was not so sure that mind and matter were completely separated, because God might have given matter the power to think (Duns Scotus had the same thought about four centuries earlier). That thought may excite motion he considered as undeniable, though incomprehensible. He agreed that minds were affected by external stimuli, but, and this was his chief contribution, he believed that there were no "innate" ideas—(ideas born in the mind or created by the mind without aid from outside); he thought that every idea must be the result of some *experience*, and that experience was of two kinds—sensation and reflection. The experience due to sensation was that got from outside the mind through the organs of sense, while that due to reflection was the result of the mind reflecting "on its own operations within itself," that is, experiencing its own thoughts,

Leibnitz, in criticising Locke, pointed out that with regard to reflection, what was reflected upon must be in the mind *before* it could be experienced, and such a thing could not be if there were no innate ideas, for as far as the saying goes, "that there is nothing in the understanding that was not first in the senses," one exception must be made—the understanding itself. With regard to sensation, he asked how could Locke prove that the objects which caused us to have sensations did actually exist outside us? And how did we get the idea of "cause," since nobody could ever experience a cause by itself, apart from the other factors involved; or how did we get the idea of bodies existing on their own apart from anybody thinking about them, seeing that experience of them was lacking?

Although Locke could not prove the existence of a real material world outside the mind, yet he agreed with the thinkers of his day in taking a real mathematical and mechanical world for granted; he further thought that the bodies composing that world had primary qualities, such as solidity, extension, shape, motion, rest, number, etc. (all such as are mathematical or mechanical), and that these gave rise to secondary qualities, such as colour, sound, taste, etc., but that the latter were not real on their own account; and he had to explain in some way or other how ideas of such unreal things could arise from sensation, since that which affects the senses must at least be real. He imagined that the ideas of secondary qualities were due to the senses being affected by minute and insensible parts of bodies (primary), which parts themselves bore no resemblance to the secondary qualities, but nevertheless produced the effects of colour, warmth, and so on.

We may see how he came by the latter notion if we bear in mind that Bacon had revived the idea of atoms, after the manner of Democritus, and had been followed in that by many other students in the field of natural science. The theories based on atoms offered a better groundwork for an explanation of natural processes, though at the same time they tended to do away with the apparent solid reality of matter. So just as material science had, during the Renaissance, tended to do away with theological explanations and the Supreme Mind, so did atomistic chemistry *tend to undermine the reality of matter itself,* inasmuch as one could think of matter being split up to infinity so that it could not be sense perceived in any way.

Locke, as stated, had availed himself of the atomists' way of looking at things, in order to account for ideas of secondary qualities *on the basis of sensation.* If we remember that, and also that the age was becoming materialistic, we shall be in a better position to understand why George Berkeley, a bishop, interested in upholding the idea of spirituality, supported Locke's teaching that knowledge is due to sensation, but attacked his distinction between primary and secondary qualities. The reason was because he thought Locke's materialist and mechanistic arguments would, if carried to their logical conclusion, result in smashing the very materialism they were intended to support.

BERKELEY (1685—1753, of Dysert, Kilkenny— Bishop of Cloyne, in Ireland) allowed that knowledge was derived from ideas of sensation, which ideas, of course, were in the mind, but did not see the necessity for anything outside the mind; in fact, did not see how we could form a conception of any such thing, because what was perceived was an idea *in the mind*, and an idea was something different from the supposed object outside. Nor could such an object, assuming there to be one, think like our own minds, for it was precisely on that basis that we distinguished between mind and matter. Whatever could the object be? Locke had said that it was something solid, heavy, etc., but not coloured or heated; these secondary qualities being no more than effects produced on the senses. But how, Berkeley asked, could Locke know this? How could he tell that ideas of primary qualities resembled objects while those of secondary qualities did not, when the only contact with the outside source of ideas was by means of the ideas themselves? Again, if the nature of any outside object was different from the nature of an idea (matter different from mind), and ideas alone could be perceived, how could an idea resemble it? And if it did, how could we imagine it apart from the secondary qualities of warmth, colour, etc., which Locke had said it did not really possess?

Berkeley concluded that outside objects did not exist. In reply to Dr. Johnson's kicking a stone by way of refuting that conclusion, he admitted everything to which the senses bore witness, but denied that anything existed apart from the actual sense perceptions; for the very being or existence of all things that were perceived *lay in them being perceived.* He therefore denied the existence of matter. Asked what became of matter when it was not being perceived, he replied, it did not exist; because the idea of existence always meant existence as an object of perception. To think of an object unperceived was really thinking of it being perceived, *without the notion of a person perceiving it.*

Now, such ideas as the last, which are framed at will, namely, all kinds of suppositions, he called "ideas of imagination." But ideas that did not depend upon our willing, for example, those of gravity causing bodies to fall or fire causing a burn, and so on, he called "ideas of sense"; and as we could not produce such ideas at will, and as matter did not exist, and therefore could not produce them for us, ideas of sense, he thought, could only be produced by a Spirit of a higher order than ourselves (in so far as we produced ideas of imagination we were spirits of a low order), who arranged what we call the laws of nature (cause and effect, etc.), and although it was impossible to discover any *necessary* connection between those laws, nevertheless without that supposition we should be in utter confusion; so he considered it reasonable to think that the Great Spirit arranged the connection which, as we came to understand it through experience, might be regarded as the language by which the Spirit communicated with us. This was pure idealism.

Following Berkeley came DAVID HUME (1711—1776, of Edinburgh), who, while in France in 1739, wrote a "Treatise of Human Nature." Hume said, just as Berkeley treated matter as being nothing but perceptions, so ought we to treat Berkeley's Spirit also as non-existent except in our perceptions, for we knew no more of it apart from perceptions than we knew of matter apart from perceptions. To say, as Berkeley did, that proof of the existence of a superior Spirit was to be found in the connection between perceptions of cause and effect (the beautiful order in the universe) only begged the question, for that so-called connection was merely a habit of mind, the result of noticing that certain kinds of perceptions always followed certain other kinds; for even if certain ones did always follow certain others, Hume thought this might just happen so, the happening in no way proving the connection. Since Hume's time the question of whether one thing *causes* another, or whether the two just happen so without being connected, has been known as the problem of causality. So Hume was a complete sceptic —no innate ideas, no mind or Spirit, no soul, no external world or matter, nothing but perceptions which nobody understood. Hume's fellow Scotsmen could not stand that, so took to expounding the "principles of common sense"; but their work merits very little notice in an outline, where much detail must of necessity be missed.

With the ship of philosophy in such a parlous state, Immanuel Kant took the helm and sought to pilot it into safe harbour. In effect, he said, away with the lot of you, what we ought to do is to give up arriving at dogmatic positions, everyone of which seems to be knocked over by the next philosopher that happens to come along; we ought to pay no attention to the truth of the universe, the object of our study, until we first understand the tool we are using—our reason; he therefore turned away from the study of the universe itself, in order to study those faculties of reason which are employed in studying that universe.

ABSTRACT.—After ancient ideas had failed to give satisfaction, Descartes said, away with all dogma. He began with doubt *but ended with dogma.* He saw that thought existed, and from that deduced the reality of God, of the human mind and of matter. Spinoza did away with the separate mind and matter, retained God, the unity, but sacrificed individuality. Leibnitz restored individuality of mind, but not of matter. Locke restored individuality of both. Berkeley destroyed not only the individuality of parts of matter, but the whole of matter, and retained Spirit. Hume destroyed both Spirit and matter, leaving only "perceptions," but knew nothing definite about them; while the Scotch philosophers, out of breath, returned to the "principles of common sense." Through all this may be seen the gradual forming, in a broad sense, of the two modern schools—the idealists and the materialists, while the problem to be solved became definitely that of *how* we do our thinking, the solution of which was attempted by Kant.

CHAPTER VI

The Philosophy of Immanuel Kant

IMMANUEL KANT (1724—1804, of Könisberg) was the first of those German philosophers who have been called great. Though born in 1724, he did not publish his first philosophical work till 1781; his philosophy is accordingly late eighteenth century. In this chapter we outline his three chief works—the three Critiques.

When Hume had reduced the dogmas of previous philosophers to scepticism, and had denied the connection between cause and effect by saying that causes did not exist except in our minds, Kant thought it high time to cease dogmatising. He therefore attempted a critical enquiry into the nature of our reasoning faculty, for the purpose of finding out how far our reason was capable of forming correct ideas.

It was Hume's problem of causality that led Kant to his basic conception, which is that just as the movement of the sun in the heavens is only an apparent motion due to our way of looking at it, so are the positions and shapes of bodies *in space*, and the succession of events as they follow *in time*, only appearances due to the peculiar nature of our perceiving faculties.

Hume had followed Locke in supposing there were no innate ideas, that is, that the mind could produce no ideas at all without the aid of experience, but Kant thought the mind *could* produce such ideas, for example, those of the mathematical kind, which cannot be experienced for the simple reason that no such exactness can be found in nature; therefore, according to him, mathematical truths *must* be produced *à priori*, which means without experience, or prior to experience. But since all knowledge, of whatever kind, must be knowledge of something that is extended *in space* (that has some sort of shape, and is therefore geometrical), or knowledge of some event in time (which involves the use of numbers in calculation), all knowledge must, to that extent, be mathematical; so it follows that all knowledge of the universe, or of its separate parts, must be made up of two portions, the *à priori* ideas or mathematical parts contributed by the mind itself without the aid of experience, in addition to *à posteriori* ideas, namely, those contributed through the experience of our organs of sense.

Such knowledge is wholly in the mind, but not in Berkeley's sense, because Kant held the view that ideas in the mind were merely the mental pictures of *how things appeared to us,* that is, they were only *appearances* or phenomena, and since there could be no appearance without something to appear, there must, he thought, be a world of things outside our minds with which we could never come face to face, nor could we ever come face to face with our minds themselves, we only knew the *à priori* ideas contained in them or produced by them. Therefore the world of things including our minds, though only in so far as our experience could take us, was something real " in itself," this he called a noumenon; but we could never know that "thing in itself," for we could never get in touch with anything beyond inside sense perceptions of the things that were outside us (things in themselves), in addition to the purely mental concepts of space and time relating to those perceptions (and therefore limited by them), namely, the mathematical parts of knowledge which were produced by the mind itself. Accordingly all understanding consists of the union of two kinds of experienced *phenomena,* one supplied by sense perception, the other by the mind *prior* to its being experienced.

Those parts of understanding supplied by the mind Kant called "constitutive" notions, or categories, because they arranged the sense perceptions into different categories or classes of knowledge, for without such arrangement the sense perceptions would not constitute knowledge. Were there no faculty of understanding, perception could make nothing of what was perceived, while, on the other hand, understanding, without sense perceptions, would have nothing to understand. The sense perceptions were the variable elements, while the constitutives or categories were the constant elements (akin to Plato's Forms), and were classed under four heads—Quality, Quantity, Relation and Modality; these were the pure forms or "notions of the understanding." For example, take the notion of cause, which comes under the head of Relation, and imagine that the senses supply the mind with the perception of a blow being struck with a hammer, and another perception of the sound which follows; there is no separate perception of the blow *causing* the sound, the mind supplies the latter part of the idea, and thereby establishes a *relation* between the two perceptions, enabling them to be understood. The notion of Relation may, of course, be applied to thousands of *different* and variable combinations of perceptions, itself remaining the *constant* or invariable element enabling us to understand those different combinations. In this way Kant unified under one head or category numerous dissimilar elements.

Understanding might be called reason in an *impure* state, that is, mixed up with sense perceptions. To the extent of this combination the external world, or noumenon, including our minds, *is real*, even though we never can get at it "in itself"; but if our minds attempt to transcend these limits, where, for the lack of experienced sense perceptions no proper knowledge is possible, they go into the realm of mere ideas without any substantial backing, ideas which do not represent reality; so, there being no sense perceptions to classify, the notions are not constitutive, and not being any longer connected with the physical are accordingly metaphysical. Though in so far as such notions lead us to acquire more experience, and consequent real knowledge, so do they direct or regulate us; but since

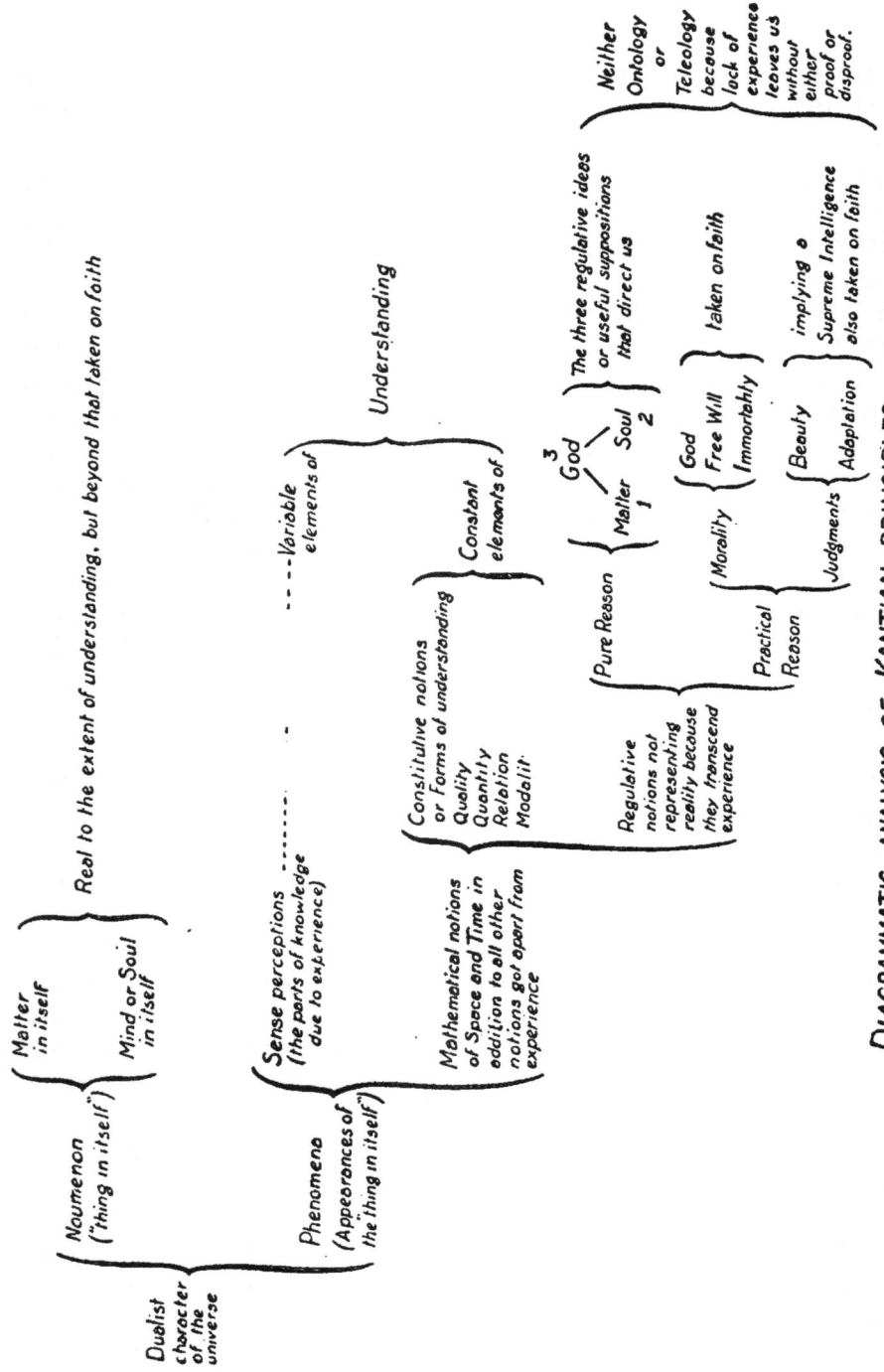

DIAGRAMMATIC ANALYSIS OF KANTIAN PRINCIPLES.

Dualist character of the universe:

- **Noumenon** ("thing in itself")
  - Matter in itself
  - Mind or Soul in itself

  } Real to the extent of understanding, but beyond that taken on faith

- **Phenomena** (Appearances of the "thing in itself")
  - Sense perceptions (the parts of knowledge due to experience) — — — Variable elements of Understanding
  - Mathematical notions of Space and Time in addition to all other notions got apart from experience
    - Constitutive notions or Forms of understanding: Quality, Quantity, Relation, Modality } Constant elements of Understanding
  - Regulative notions not representing reality because they transcend experience
    - **Pure Reason**: Matter¹, Soul², God³ } The three regulative ideas or useful suppositions that direct us
    - **Practical Reason**:
      - Morality { God, Free Will, Immortality } taken on faith
      - Judgments { Beauty, Adaptation } implying a Supreme Intelligence also taken on faith
    - } Neither Ontology or Teleology because lack of experience leaves us without either proof or disproof.

these "regulative" notions are wholly detached from experienced sense perceptions, they constitute reason apart from understanding; in other words, they constitute "pure reason."

"CRITIQUE OF PURE REASON" (1781). So long as regulative ideas do not go beyond the range of a possible experience, they may lead us to knowledge whenever the experience should take place, but reason without that experience can never produce real knowledge. It is on this account that metaphysics can never be a science; nevertheless pure reason cannot help speculating metaphysically. That being so, since constitutive notions of the understanding have already unified sense perceptions into different degrees of unity (the different categories), pure reason now goes on to imagine, first, a complete unity of all material things, that is, a material universe, though the understanding, for lack of complete experience, can never grasp it: second, a unity of all thoughts, sensations passions, etc., in short, all mental things, or a soul, though again the understanding can never grasp it; and third, a still higher unity of the first and the second, the greatest unity of all, which is God.

Owing to its nature, our reason cannot help raising these problems, but also owing to its nature it cannot solve them. They are Kant's three "regulative" Ideas, though this time not like Plato's, because they lack that definite reality. They must not be confused with Ontology, because even though pure reason cannot think otherwise than that such unities exist, this is no proof that they do so exist apart from our thinking, it only proves that we think that way. As already said, these ideas are not in the realm of knowledge, so they can only be in that of faith, wherein Kant said we have sufficient grounds for acting as though God existed and that we have immortal souls and free wills; sufficient grounds for treating those ideas as *moral* certainties, though not *demonstrated* certainties. But since these moral certitudes are expressed in action, reason ceases to be merely theoretical and becomes practical, so for Kant's explanation of why such ideas should be treated as representing something morally certain we must turn to his account of reason as applied in practice.

"CRITIQUE OF PRACTICAL REASON" (1788). Reason as applied to practical affairs means that those affairs are considered and judged, in virtue of which our conduct is directed. Practical reason is, therefore, only another name for the human will in action. Every *considered* action is taken in reference to some scheme of conduct, in answer to the questions, what shall I do in this case, or in that? With regard to the different individual cases, each has its own reason; but when it comes to doing one's duty, this applies *to all men,* even though it be executed individually; and in Kant's opinion this moral obligation to do one's duty is found *in the knowledge each one has of what is right,* and which requires obedience to what Kant called the "categorical imperative." The latter may be described as the imperious or commanding voice of conscience which commands us to do what we know to be right, irrespective of whether we like to or not.

Now why did philosophers pay so much attention to morality? When we remember that economic conditions prior to the sixteenth century had produced the Reformation and the consequent dethronement of the Catholic Church as the source of direction in moral conduct, and when we also remember that for another two centuries the economic forces had brought into prominence the new manufacturing class, *with its own ideas of what was right,* as opposed to those of the Nobility, a development that culminated in the French Revolution of 1789, we can easily understand the type of moral reflex which showed itself during this period. Not knowing the roots of moral reflexes, they imagined morality to be wholly a product of the mind, and, having thrown the more extreme theologians with their supreme mind overboard, had necessarily to attack the problem themselves, for it would never do to leave the world without moral guidance. It has even been supposed that the newer type of thinking produced the French Revolution. However that may be, and we shall see later, during the seventeenth and eighteenth centuries there had been a great number of books on moral philosophy, wherein each writer tried to show the basis of right action. Hobbes had made morality to a great extent synonymous with obedience to the laws of the State. Cudworth (1617—1688) and Clark (1675—1729) said that true morality, like mathematics, was independent of the will of either God or man, it was something true in itself. The third Earl of Shaftesbury (1671—1713) and Francis Hutcheson (1694—1747, a Scottish professor) thought that morality turned upon our possession of a natural capacity, a sentiment or inward taste that enabled us to discriminate between good and bad. Hume (1711—1776) agreed with the two latter that morality depended upon sentiment rather than reason, but added the idea of utility, so that additional satisfaction was derived from having done something useful. Adam Smith (1723—1790) thought we ought to do what we would think other people ought to do under similar circumstances in case we were impartial spectators. Joseph Butler (1692—1752, Bishop of Durham) held to the "manifest authority" of conscience, tempered by a "reasonable self love," so thought that duty to oneself ought to be considered as well as duty to one's neighbour. Butler, along with Richard Price (1723—1791, a dissenting minister), were more like Kant than the others, in that they made reason rather than sentiment the basis of morality, but Kant differed more or less from each of the foregoing by insisting on the *unconditional* aspect of his "categorical imperative."

As already explained, his "regulative notions" are unconditioned by experience, because we never have such experience, they are imaginary goals of knowledge at which we aim; but he insists that there is a great difference between the theoretical aspect of those notions and the "categorical imperative" (the voice of conscience), which is also unconditioned, because the latter brings us into relation with other human beings, it is so strong and manifest throughout society that we cannot get away from it; therefore it has a practical value over and above the merely theoretical aspect of regulative notions, so that to do one's duty irrespective of anything else is the highest of all human aims. Aristotle had said knowledge was the highest goal. Neoplatonists and Scholastics had thought it should be the "beatific vision" (the ultimate union, or at least communion with God). To Spinoza it was an intellectual love of God. But though the tendency in Germany in Kant's time was to look to knowledge as the superior aim, Kant turned away from this because it was only possible for the few, whereas the performance of duty was within the reach of all (even the ignorant peasant, whose "duty" was rapidly taking the form of working for the rising capitalist class, because with Kant, "what was right" meant what was right for this class). He stuck to Reason as the basis of morality to such an extent as to imply that one could be sure that duty was the motive, only when that duty was performed in defiance of personal interest and inclination; he also implied that a duty that was at the same time a pleasure could not be performed from a purely right motive. In nothing was he more insistent than that in our *moral* judgments it was not feeling or emotion, but solely the principle of reason, that was active. Moreover, it was an individual affair, for if a man did not obey *his own* conscience his acts were not truly moral, and, since it was as a *reasoning being* that he made his decision, so did it become necessary to treat other people as being also capable of that reason which implies the necessary freedom for its exercise, because in being aware of the moral law, so is every individual aware also that his will seems to be free; for when he knows he ought to do certain things, he has no doubt that he can both "will" them and do them. From this follows, first, the idea of individual freedom; second, that we recognise the equal freedom of other reasoning beings; and third, the idea of a community of such beings bound together by the consciousness of their obligation to keep the same law.

We have now reached the philosophical expression, or reflex, of those material developments (obtaining in

THINKING

other countries besides France) that brought about the French Revolution, and it should be interesting to notice also the close parallel between the philosophic and the political forms of thinking arising from the same conditions.

PHILOSOPHIC.	POLITICAL.	
1. Free will for the individual.	1. Liberty.	*The watchwords*
2. Free will for others also.	2. Equality.	*of the French*
3. Community among such free wills.	3. Fraternity.	*Revolution.*

So, Kant would argue, the freedom of the will is implied by morality, and morality appears to be in obedience to the imperious command of reason. But since the will *precedes action,* it cannot be experienced by the senses, only the results can be so experienced; and since there can be no knowledge apart from experience, it follows that we can never be positive that we have free wills while all the time we are compelled to act as though we have. He dealt similarly with Immortality and God, for we are compelled to go on in a seemingly continual advance towards an ideal which we can never imagine ourselves as attaining (the ideal perfection of the Soul), and also we are compelled to imagine a ruler of the world, in whose government of it morality is the chief consideration. But though there is no proof of either God, Freedom or Immortality, neither is there disproof; they remain objects of faith. The sufficient grounds for belief Kant found in the thought that without such faith our whole moral life would have no meaning. Therefore, the "categorical imperative" in the every-day life of all men, as compared with the pursuit of knowledge by the few, distinguishes the moral or "practical" side of a "regulative" idea, which compels us to obey, from the speculative or "theoretical" side, which merely directs our endeavour to acquire knowledge.

"CRITIQUE OF THE FACULTY OF JUDGMENT." In addition to the phenomena already considered, Kant dealt with two other kinds—beauty and adaptation. concerning which his thought ran along the following lines. When thinking of the beauty of an object in nature, we cannot avoid considering it as the work of an intelligence, though greater than that of any human being, much in the same way that when admiring a beautiful statue we think of the intelligence of the artist who produced it. Or, with regard to adaptation, we may think of the intelligence of the draughtsman who designs a machine, the parts of which are adapted to each other, in virtue of which they all function as one whole; but in considering the human body with its wonderful adaptation of parts, such that no human mechanic could ever devise or even explain satisfactorily on mechanical lines, we again cannot avoid thinking of such an organism as being the work of an intelligence greater than our own. At first sight this looks like Anaxagoras' or Aristotle's " teleology," but it is not, for though *we* cannot explain such things without the supposition of a superhuman " will," we are not justified in going the length of saying *they could not* have come into existence without that " will " or " design "; because even though the supposition is necessary, we must not forget that they are *only appearances,* and consequently we cannot know the cause " in itself," for we never get in touch with it, and so can never claim definite knowledge of it.

ABSTRACT.—Descartes had separated the Supreme Mind from matter and had then built an ontological bridge across the gulf. Kant destroyed that dogmatic bridge, but left a bridge of faith in things that could neither be proved or disproved. For Kant, there is a real mind, which knows only its own appearances, along with the appearances of a world, which also is real, but it can never know either itself or that real world as they are " in themselves." This real mind operates with sense perceptions of phenomena on the one hand, and its own *à priori* notions which are applicable to those sense perceptions on the other; to this extent it understands. Outside this limited experience the mind operates with its own pure reason, which, for the lack of sense-perceived phenomena, can never reach positive knowledge or what he calls understanding. Reason, in its pure state, consists of theoretical or metaphysical speculation. Reason, when applied in practice, takes the form of morality on the one hand, and certain classes of judgments on the other; the bases for both (free will and an intelligent designer of the universe) being taken on faith, while the basis for faith itself is found in the necessity for men to live a moral life. Kant did not arrive at unity like his predecessors; he was a dualist, because he believed in a world of appearances or phenomena, and also in a world or noumenon that lay for ever at the back of phenomena, and which constituted the " thing in itself." Descartes and his followers gradually brought about the modern distinction between mind and matter. Kant recognised both, but left the problem of their ultimate nature (noumena) alone. He turned his attention to the faculty of reason (phenomena), which at this point includes understanding, and so opened the way to the problem of thinking or understanding considered apart from the things that had to be thought about or understood. He did not solve the problem of understanding, but made a remarkable contribution towards formulating it correctly. The problem is not how do we understand other things, but how to understand the understanding itself. The latter question settled, the former disappears.

CHAPTER VII

Idealism from Kant to Bergson

Prior to Kant's time there had been growing up the doctrine that human reason should be the guide in all matters; that if man would cease to trust in theological dogma and rely on himself he would not go astray, for if things are logical to the mind they must be real in nature, and therefore reason must be the faculty by which man discovers truth. This is Rationalism. But Kant gave the **deathblow** to rationalism by showing that reason by itself could never produce knowledge, because it lacked experience; and surely this was amply shown in the philosophical strife we have already seen. Kant thereby showed that metaphysics was impossible as a science. On the other hand, particularly in France, there had also been growing up a narrow mechanical materialism, which attempted to explain all mental processes from the interaction of ponderable matter, a doctrine that, of course, left no opening for faith in the supernatural. But Kant refuted this as well, by teaching that reason alone could produce "regulative" notions amounting to moral certainties, namely, those of God, Immortality and Freedom. So faith, with its cardinal principle of freedom, was reinstated. This shows Kant to be the philosopher of the rising manufacturing or middle class, the Liberals or the bourgeoisie, as they are called, who required freedom from the power of the landlord class.

Kant's influence was so great that the philosophy which preceded him fell into the background, at least in Germany, and his doctrine that understanding can never know the "thing in itself," while all the time it is limited by it, underlay the work of many who succeeded him, for example, Comte, who limited human science to *external* phenomena, and this only within the solar system, thus excluding the science of mind— psychology, and the science of the stars—sidereal astronomy. It also underlay the theory of the "relativity of knowledge" taught by Sir W. Hamilton (1788 —1856, of Glasgow, later Edinburgh University) and H. L. Mansel (1820—1871, of Cosgrove, Northamptonshire, Dean of St. Paul's); and in a different way by Herbert Spencer, who insisted on the limitations of knowledge in order to leave no room for faith in supernatural revelation. These relativists did not rely so much upon the *nature* of our thinking faculties, as upon the fact that all knowledge *must consist in a relation* between a mind which knows and some object which is known; in other words, a "subject" and an "object." Of course, the existence or recognition of this relation does not do away with the question of whether a thing as it appears to us differs from the "thing in itself" apart from our sense perceptions, and Kant was not without opponents concerning his dualism of noumenon and phenomena. One line of thinkers, who developed the more modern forms of idealism, sprang from that side of Kant which dealt with phenomena, and for the present we are concerned with explaining the chief points in that development.

JOHANN GOTLIEB FICHTE (1762—1814, of Rammenau, Jena, and Berlin) thought there was no need to trouble about a "thing in itself." In his opinion there was only one thing, and that was mind, which, so to speak, divided itself into two in order that the subject, the part that knows, might have an object to think about; but this was not an individual mind, it was the mind of the world, or mind in general. Berkeley thought that so-called external objects were only ideas of individual spirits, but Fichte conceived the notion that *all that existed* consisted of one total mind, which included all the things we know, as well as that which knows them. It was an "absolute self." But he, like others, was troubled with the question of morality, and concluded that this total mind split itself in two, in order that one part, that which knows, judges and decides, might use the other part, usually called nature, as an obstacle to be overcome so that the first part could demonstrate its moral character by performing the duty of overcoming nature. He also thought that the second part, or nature, acted as a means of communication between individuals, for the total mind included many individual selves, so that each could practice morality in executing duties to others. With Fichte this complete moral order constituted an " absolute self," which might be called God, and to him there was no other God. His " absolute " was the complete unity of so-called matter and so-called mind, and was limited to what was " in relation," that is, as between knower and known, or subject and object; but it was all mind, there was no matter in itself, the part called matter was regarded as subordinate, and only existed for the other part called mind to play upon.

FRIEDRICH WILHELM JOSEPH von SCHELLING (1775—1854, of Leonberg, in Würtemburg, and Universities of Jena, Munich, Berlin, etc.) differed from Fichte in that he thought of an ultimate reality which underlay both mind and so-called matter, though without any definite character of its own; we never got face to face with it, but knew of it by a kind of intuition. He further thought that nature was not subordinate to mind, that is, utilised by the mind for itself to practice morality, because the beauty and design to be found in nature indicated that it was something more than a mere object on which to practice. He therefore conceived the existence of an " absolute something," which, though underlying the relation between that which knows and that which is known, was really outside the relation; that it had an independent reality of its own. Where Fichte's " absolute " consisted of the moral order involved in the relation between knower and known, Schelling's was something wider, a weird kind of God lying outside mind and matter, though permeating both.

Since mind and matter were both mental, Schelling's work was really an attempt to construct a trinity with the human mind as the basis, and arose from the struggle involved in explaining matter in terms of mind.

Schelling was followed by GEORG WILHELM FRIEDRICH HEGEL (1770—1831, of Stuttgart, Jena and Berlin), who thought that Schelling's "absolute" was altogether too vague. It took no notice of the connection between mind and matter, which comes into play when we are reflecting about so-called material things, which reflection is the common experience of everybody. He thought that in ordinary daily reflection and discussion, men were actually engaged in tracing out the structure of what he called the Absolute Idea. With Hegel the Absolute is not something in the background, except that part of it that has not yet been discovered; on the contrary, its very being is *in* the manifestations of the life and movement of mind and so-called matter. This complete and permanent Idea had existed from all eternity and as men struggled with their problems, found themselves in contradictions, discovered new knowledge which explained or solved the contradictions, and in this way kept advancing, so were they ever more and more coming to a knowledge of the complete Idea, the Absolute.

Hegel agreed that the mind in its advancing required a so-called material world with which it could strive, but that material world was with him only another part of the Idea, in other words, it was mental; all the advancing, then, consisted of the Idea gradually unfolding itself, and was, in fact, simply the evolution of the Idea. This evolution, which appeared in our minds as a kind of argument in which conflicting statements were ultimately reconciled in a conclusion, was a revival of dialectics. In it our whole life appears to be *constantly changing,* so that every conclusion in the argument is but a new starting point in another argument that is to end in a still higher conclusion, and so are we ever attaining greater and greater unity, more and more truth.

But how are we to recognise truth or reality at any given time amid all this change? Kant had said that the mathematical parts of knowledge existed in the mind, but not in the things. Hegel asked how could that be? If truth were not in the things, then all our science is illusion; for example, gravity and the laws of motion. Rather is it that the thing which appears *is the reality itself appearing* and not something else; and further, if this appearance seems to be reasonable or rational, consistent or logical, it *must* be real, and being real must be rational, for *how could we understand what is not real?* How shall we know the real and true, except by the fact that it is intelligible, understandable, rational, reasonable, logical, consistent? Hegel's test of truth, therefore, is that which is reasonable and logical to the mind; for example, to test whether or not our writing desks are real we must touch them, because it is reasonable to test such things by the senses, but to test whether the Idea (God) is real or not, it is reasonable to rely on the "ontological argument," but unreasonable to submit such an idea of *intelligibility* to the senses; therefore, the truth of all things may be brought to light by putting reasonable questions to oneself or to other people, and as different conclusions are arrived at by this reasoning process, so are we tracing out bit by bit the structure of reality, which is God or the Absolute, and there is no other Absolute.

This method of enquiry, as stated, is dialectic, because it takes the form of an argument, whereby we may find truth at any given time amid *a constant flow* of historical development. In applying it Hegel had at his command a much wider knowledge of history than had Plato, consequently the dialectic in his hands came to be of great significance as a method of interpreting history; it constituted his great contribution to modern progress in scientific thinking, for by means of it he propounded the nature of the problem to be solved, namely, the discovery of the law underlying the changes which have taken place in history, or, in short, the law of human progress, and also the method of solving it. He fell short, however, in the actual solution.

Since the dialectic method deals with a constant flow from one thing to another, or, rather, the evolution of one thing out of that which preceded it, it must, of course, consider *the relation* between opposite terms of a contradiction. In the realm of morality it takes into account not only Kant's " categorical imperative," or what *ought* to be, but also *what is* when it might seem to contradict what ought to be. For example, starting from the thought that man has a free will, how can we justify the idea of law, which is the negation or contradiction of freedom? First take the idea that a man is free to do what he likes with his property. When this man enters into relations with other similarly free men, each has to recognise the rights of the others, consequently personal freedom, which was real and true originally, gets curtailed by the rise of a *reasonable* moral law, which, because reasonable, *now becomes real*, while absolute personal freedom becomes unreal or untrue. This greater unity we may assume, in the first place, to take the form of the family, then, with further development, a wider form in social groups of many families, and a still wider form in the State, until, in the end, the mind finds itself in its highest stage, which is realised, not only in the idea of the State, but also that of the Monarchy; so that as society develops, personal freedom, which at one time was reasonable, and therefore real or true, becomes at a later stage unreasonable or unreal, and no longer true. In this way, through reconciling the contradictions by combining all the historical factors, Hegel proves that, taken altogether, *what is,* at any given time, *is what ought to be,* and if it ought to be, then it is reasonable and accordingly real.

To Hegel the continual change which has taken place throughout history, and is still taking place, is nothing less than the dialectic being acted. It is the Idea unfolding itself in its march towards its complete unfolding—the Absolute Idea, and only in such a way could the unfolding take place. (This talking of an absolute *end* alongside perpetual *change* is a contradiction that is unreconcilable.) It appears as a conflict between the wills of different men or groups of men who argue or contend for their particular parts of reality. They each get their corners rubbed off, and out of the contradictory parts comes a reconciliation which is seen by most people to be reasonable, it is therefore real because it is intelligible, logical or consistent. However, later, new contradictions arise, followed by different reconciliations, and of course a different reality; so the older reality is no longer reasonable and becomes unreal, its place being occupied by the newly and more widely reasonable. It must be remembered that all this takes place in the mind, the so-called material world is only a sort of image in the mind of that part of the Absolute Idea which appears as nature in order that the complete mind shall carry out its destiny. Therefore, reality or truth is constantly changing, what is true at one time is untrue at another, because mind has advanced in the meantime and discovered an additional part of absolute truth which modifies the previous reality and therefore negates it; a still further advance would in like manner negate the previous negation, and so on and on continually until the complete Idea has been unfolded, but meanwhile *what is at any given moment is what ought to be.* Is it any wonder the tyrannical Prussian Government of Hegel's day welcomed such a comforting philosophy?

Just as Kant's doctrine of freedom was the philosophy of the middle class since it voiced their need for " liberty, equality and fraternity," so, thirty years later, Hegel's doctrine that " what is, is what ought to be " was simply a philosophical expression of the same material conditions when the middle class had got what they wanted and were crying halt; but to get the full force of this it is necessary to remember that prior to the French Revolution of 1789, the Liberals, or manufacturing element, needed freedom from the restrictions imposed on them by the landed nobility, though they were not powerful enough to get it without the aid of the lower class of working people. At the time of the Revolution the two classes (middle class and working class) had carried all before them, the working class thought they had conquered liberty, and so they had, but not for themselves, for as soon as the nobility were overthrown and their power broken, the middle class had got all the freedom they required and had no wish to share it with the working class. They, the middle class, were to be the new master class, it was therefore dangerous to allow liberty to the working class whom they were to exploit. The march towards liberty had gone far enough for them, so they called a halt and eventually restored the Monarchy, though in a limited form. Hegel's doctrine, then, was a mental reflex of the period of restoration, while that of Kant represented the period of attack. Kant's was a war cry for freedom, Hegel's was a hymn of thanksgiving that things had reached a *settled state*. But here came the contradiction that ruined Hegel's philosophy, for his method was dialectic (changing), his system static (settled).

Hegel's philosophy had a short but brilliant run. His followers ultimately split into two camps. The right wing clung to the static side, believing that " what is, is what ought to be "; this, we have seen, was pleasing to the Prussian Government. But that same Government's " unjust " taxation, harsh laws and refusal to allow to the German middle class any democratic voice in government, led to the formation of the left wing, known as the Young Hegelians. The left wing accepted the dialectical part of Hegel but rejected the static, and in the hands of Marx and Engels, who sprang from the Young Hegelians, and later, Dietzgen, the dialectical view led for the first time to scientific results in thinking, because it constituted the method employed, or rather the view taken, in building up the science of society.

Meanwhile there were wars, misery and seemingly nothing but angry contention. When all the philosophers one after the other had tried to solve the question of what was moral, right, just, etc., it appeared that things were worse than ever. This was the state of affairs that gained a hearing for ARTHUR SCHOPENHAUER (1788—1860, of Dantzig, Berlin and Frankfort-on-Main), who, like Hegel, took his root notion of the human will from Kant. But while Hegel thought the will was merely the means by which the mind struggled with nature and found out the real good in the Idea, Schopenhauer thought *it was the only thing that existed*; but, in order to express itself, it divided itself into " will " (the reality that strives to attain its desires) on the one hand, and " knowledge " (its own creation) on the other. The will, he thought, employed knowledge for the mere purpose of expressing its own desire as " the will to live." But he further thought the will *was essentially bad*; and the only good that came out of all the striving was that the reason *ultimately became aware* that complete satisfaction cannot be attained, and therefore the best thing to do is to give up striving, to renounce all interest in any satisfaction to be got in life, and to calmly await death. It reminds one of certain aspects of Buddhism and Theosophy.

However, the material conditions still continued to throw up their mental reflexes. After the German and French Revolutions of 1848 and 1852, capital was producing wealth, vice and luxury at the top of society, and poverty, vice and misery at the bottom; little men here and there were struggling to become capitalists, small capitalists struggling to become greater capitalists while the great ones had already entered on the struggle to determine which particular group should become world dominant; it was more than ever the era of competitive struggle resulting from the enormously-increased *machine* production and the consequent cross investments of capital tending towards the unification of ownership of tools and materials. The better tools caused an overproduction of certain classes of goods and led to fierce international competition for markets. All this fierce struggle was expressed philosophically by FRIEDRICH NIETZSCHE (1844—1900, of Röcken and Basel) who imagined that those who resigned themselves to their fate deserved nothing better, for the human " will to live," if rightly understood, **was** not a bad thing, but, on the contrary, the best thing we possessed; and far from despondently waiting for death, we ought to be continually working with might and main to develop those dominant qualities whereby in the struggle for existence more vigorous races would be produced, men who would be as far above the men of to-day as the latter are above the beasts; this became known as the doctrine of the Superman. Here, again, the advance of science was reflected in philosophy, for in 1859 Darwin had published the results of his biological researches in which he expounded his doctrine of the " origin of species " by " natural selection " and " the survival of the fittest."

During the century preceding Nietzsche's philosophy, Kant and his German followers, as already stated, had treated the mind as capable of producing ideas without the aid of the senses, but it took a long time for this to affect English thought. Englishmen for a couple of centuries had been materialists, developing in the main along the lines laid down by Bacon, Hobbes and Locke, namely, that truth was to be sought by studying nature, and that ideas could not be produced except by means of sensation. They sought to account for ideas by the same method as that used in explaining nature, and treated ideas as being made up, so to speak, of mental atoms. They tried to explain mental work as the " association of ideas," and sought to find the laws of that association. For example, Hume explained the notion of a cause as being composed of, or built up from, often repeated associations of a particular kind. These men were known as the " EMPIRICAL PSYCHOLOGISTS" and include David Hartly (1705—1757, of Halifax), James Mill (1773—1836, of Northwater Bridge, in Forfarshire, later London), John Stuart Mill (1806—1873, of London, son of James Mill), and Alexander Bain (1818—1903, Prof. of Logic at Aberdeen). Between Hartly and J. Mill there were Thomas Reid (1710—1796, of Strachan, Kincardineshire; succeeded Adam Smith in Glasgow as Moral Philosopher) and Dugald Stewart (1753—1828, of Edinburgh), who founded the Scottish school, of which Sir W. Hamilton was a leading light; the general feature of this school was a confidence in common-sense and intuitive convictions, which made them opponents of all forms of philosophic scepticism.

If we remember that philosophers had thrown theological direction in moral matters overboard and were still searching for the origin of morality in the human mind, we shall see it to be only natural that those who tried to explain all forms of thought as being due to sensation should attempt to explain morality as arising from a combination of the feelings of pleasure and pain; and in this way arose the school of Utilitarianism represented by JEREMY BENTHAM (1747—1832, of London) and JOHN S. MILL. When asked to explain the idea of "virture *for its own sake*" on the basis of utilitarianism, they thought it arose from the "association of ideas" wherein a man who had learned by experience that he got most pleasure by being virtuous, gradually got into the habit of being virtuous, so that the practice of virtue, which originally had been only a means of attaining pleasure, eventually came to be the end in view. However, this is a view developed from the standpoint *of an individual,* it does not explain that conviction which most people have of there being a "right" which is right *for everybody*; nor does it explain the so-called universal mathematical truths. Herbert Spencer suggested that the latter ideas might be accounted for by assuming that our ancestors had had the experience necessary to form the ideas, and that our inherent convictions had been handed down to us through heredity; but this was no explanation, for whichever way we look at it, no amount of *individual* experience, however far back, could account for what is *absolutely* and *universally* true, because no individual could ever experience something that is universal.

By degrees, however, English sensationalism came to be influenced by German idealism. THOMAS HILL GREEN (1836—1882, of Birkin, in Yorkshire, and Oxford University), who pointed out that Hume had long ago reduced the sensation theory to scepticism, was a student of Kant and Hegel; he called attention to the fact that the objects of natural science which were outside the mind could not be reduced to a combination of feelings; nor could a common or *universal* " good " or " happiness " or " right " be understood by individuals as being composed of their feelings in total since their feelings were only momentary. Therefore, he argued, there must be, in addition to the objects outside the mind, a permanent mind to remember those feelings, and also, this mind must be capable of knowing what is always and everywhere true, it must be a universal mind, or God, of which individual minds were so-called reproductions. Others, not taking into consideration that the mind is always engaged in seeking unity, thought the universal mind was nothing but an abstraction, so they held that only individual minds need be considered. WILLIAM JAMES (1842—1910, Prof. of Phil. at Harvard) taught a theory known as " pragmatism," based on the independence of individual minds and their ability to arrive at truth by finding out what is practicable in relation to individual interests. Altogether, an idealist strain gradually permeated English materialism, but in the latter part of the nineteenth century there were reversions which showed themselves in what has been called " realism," though with a different meaning as compared with the realism of the Scholastics.

Realism, a reflex of German materialism, is really a dualism of matter and force, of which we shall see more in the next chapter. This dualism, added to the doctrine of evolution, found expression in HERBERT SPENCER'S " Synthetic Philosophy," wherein he attempted to show by the " persistence of force " the evolution from atoms to societies. The concept of biological evolution when applied to society, treats society as a biological organism and directs philosophic thought towards the study of the biological principle of " life," as expressed *in the evolution of society;* the ever-present " urge " which drives society onward. George Bernard Shaw calls this " urge " the " life force." Since this active living principle appears to operate whether we are conscious of it or not, there arise the questions of its relation to consciousness on the one hand and to mere mechanism on the other; these questions lie at the root of modern psychology, they are the two parts of our old question as to the connection between mind and matter, because "life" is here treated *as an entity expressing itself partly in mind and partly in matter*. As far as philosophy is concerned, the whole thing put simply means that philosophers have definitely dropped the word "God" and substituted that of "Life," *but they are still where they were.*

On the idealist side, the final outburst, up to date, comes from HENRI BERGSON (Prof. at the College of France). With Bergson, truth is the life which pervades the universe, or, rather, which *is* the universe. It consists of that *general* consciousness or intuition, of which instinct (as in bees and ants) is a more highly-concentrated form, while intellect (as in man), which has evolved along a different line, is the most highly concentrated. Its essence is an eternally-changing *now,* an absolute time duration which we apprehend in intuition. This intuitive duration is identical with being or existence, for we know intuitively that we are living and this life or reality is nothing but movement, a movement of pure time. Matter is an illusion produced by part of the total movement taking place in a reverse direction to other currents, thus giving to these time currents the appearance of material objects. Material objects are, therefore, nothing but the obstacles that each current presents to the other just at the points where the *now is becoming the future.* This conception, of matter being, by illusion, the materialised impact of two time currents, is a reflex of the electron theory, wherein matter is materialised energy resulting from the impact of two electric forces that reduce each other to inertia, the electron, the base of ponderable matter, being the point of electrical inertia. In **Bergson's** working out, the different parts of consciousness act upon and therefore condition each other; so, considered as parts, are not free, but, when taken *altogether* are conditioned only by their own internal character, and consequently have a freedom. This freedom holds alike for a *whole* individual or the *whole* of life. Therefore, when we act intuitively *as a whole* we act freely; such an act is a creative act and it is such acts that constitute the evolutionary process. Creative evolution is accordingly the free surging onward of some part of universal " life " or Spirit overcoming some other part. Bergson does not offer a reconciliation of mind and matter, but rather a new view wherein the question of dualism does not arise, since they are both one life process. His followers call this reality " mind," not because it is ethereal as contrasted with gross matter, but because it is the active, living, intelligent principle of existence. In expounding this philosophy, Bergson becomes the modern mystic, his intuitive surging creation being a close parallel to the ecstacy of Plotinus.

Excluding minor differences, it should be plain that modern philosophy runs very nearly the same course as ancient philosophy; for when the Milesians with " open " minds started investigations which gave rise to problems of ultimate reality, philosophy developed its " great men," its sophists and sceptics, its dialectics, its atoms, its questions of morality wherein Epicureans based conduct upon pleasure, the Sceptics upon the common-sense of their day, the Stoics sinking back into faith while the Neoplatonists fizzled out in a state of ecstatic supernatural mysticism; and so in similar manner did modern philosophy begin with Descartes' investigations based on doubt, followed by the permanent natures of God, the scepticism of Hume, the materialism based on atomic science, the utilitarianism of Mill based on pleasure, the prior return to faith by Kant, the dialectics of Hegel, only in the end to fizzle out in the idealistic mysticism of the natural, as in Bergson and Shaw. And so must it always be, that those who start from mind without authority, end in mysticism; while those who start from mind along with authority, end in faith.

Has it been without results? No, not quite. Kant cleared the problem by showing it to be one of thinking, Hegel applied the dialectic method to a wide knowledge of history, but to see how this in the hands of Marx led to the solution of the problem of thinking, it will be necessary to go back to the seventeenth century in order to follow modern philosophy through the development of its materialist aspects.

CHAPTER VIII

Materialism from Roger Bacon to Marx

(Although some of the following points have already been mentioned in connection with other phases of the story, they are repeated in this chapter for the sake of completeness.)

Philosophic materialism originally presented itself in the form of natural philosophy, which later came to be called natural science. Positive science, in so far as any beginning can be assigned to it, appeared with ROGER BACON (1214—1294). It has been assigned to R. Bacon, notwithstanding that there had been many natural philosophers before him, because prior to his time it had been the custom in solving problems to rely for results on a process of deductive reasoning, after the manner of Aristotle. Deduction consists in taking some statement as being true and then deducing conclusions from it, but R. Bacon thought that such a method was not sufficient in itself and that we ought to take great care in establishing the first statement, or premise, for if that were false so would the conclusion be false however perfect our logic. His method was, therefore, to base all his first statements on *observed* facts, about which he formed opinions, then by deduction argued what ought to follow and finally tested his conclusions by *experimenting to* see if those conclusions *did actually follow.* This method we see at a glance to be the correct one because it tests the results obtained, which, if found not to agree with the first opinion, leads to a modification of that opinion. It consists of *observation* and *experiment,* is called the inductive method, and, along with the material investigated, forms the groundwork of all science.

DUNS SCOTUS (1274—1308), the British Schoolman and contemporary of R. Bacon, asked "Is it not possible for matter to think?" In this he made theology preach materialism by supposing that God could have produced such a miracle had he wished. He was, we remember, partly a nominalist, and nominalism which arose from natural philosophy was the first form of materialism.

Three centuries later FRANCIS BACON (1561—1626) applied the inductive method more widely in natural philosophy, so that, although not the originator of the method, as is sometimes said, he was, nevertheless, the starting point of English materialism. He sought by observation and experiment in relation to natural objects to explain the works of God. Bacon, therefore, never escaped from theistic prejudice, even though he thought that all knowledge was based on the experience of the senses. His basis was accordingly matter, but his conclusions were vitiated by a theological bias.

HOBBES (1588—1679) continued the development by reducing Bacon's teaching to something like a system. He was not disinclined to the thought of an eternal power that one might call God if it suited, but could conceive no knowledge of that God except what came to us by our senses in contact with material things; accordingly, we could know nothing about the existence of God, apart from material things. He believed that anything real must occupy space, and consequently be mathematical; also, that all changes imply motion, and must accordingly be mechanical; these two ideas were the clear and distinct notions of his contemporary, Descartes. That any other attributes of bodies, such as colour, warmth, etc., could be real he would not allow. Therefore, with him as with Descartes, the physical universe could be explained on mechanical lines. In the realm of morality, since all knowledge is due to sensation, all moral distinctions were traced to self interest. In so far as Hobbes made material the *source* of the idea of God, so did he shatter the theism of Bacon, without, however, furnishing the proof of Bacon's principle that knowledge arose from sensation.

It was JOHN LOCKE (1632—1704) (more fully treated in the fifth chapter as a background to Berkeley and Hume) who supplied the beginning of that proof. He supported the idea of sensation being the basis of knowledge, by his theory that understanding was wholly dependent on experience, but that experience was of two kinds—sensation and reflection; the reflection taking place in relation to what was in the mind as the result of sense perception (Leibnitz and Berkeley, as we have seen, criticised this position from the idealistic standpoint, see pp. 70-2). His doctrine still retained traces of theology to the extent of a belief in a Creator, since something could not come from nothing; but these were eventually dissipated by a succession of brilliant scientist—philosophers who gradually got rid of the Supreme Mind, though to this day they are confused with respect to the problem of the human mind. However, the basic thought of the sensational school remained in England, and with succeeding generations of discovery, invention and study, developed into the modern science and modern rationalism that may be typified by such names as Darwin, Huxley and Spencer. The philosophic characteristic of these thinkers has been referred to as "realism," which, as opposed to idealism of the Kantian and Hegelian types, means that external objects have a real existence; it is a product of the later nineteenth century science, whose findings were in conflict with the remains of supernaturalism, which, from the rationalists' standpoint, had to be fought, and is really a dualism of matter and force, or, in other words, it is a materialist doctrine *that was never fully worked out.* The English branch of it was in opposition to German idealism, which permeated English thought through the work of students of Kant and Hegel, but it received much support from German materialism. Therefore, since the time of Locke, the development of materialism represents a long fight between supernatural religion and idealist philosophy, on the one side, and natural science on the other, so, although it is not our purpose to follow the development of science from the standpoint of science, nevertheless, since scientific achievements have had a great effect on both religion and philosophy, they cannot be disregarded.

Before the time of Locke, Copernicus (1473—1543) had laid the base of modern astronomy with his heliocentric theory, which contradicted previous religious teaching. Vesalius (1514—1564) had made a start in the direction of modern anatomy. Gilbert (1540—1603) had discovered the principles of terrestrial magnetism. Lippershey's telescope had appeared in 1608. Galeleo (1564—1642) had contributed the principles of falling bodies, etc. Kepler (1571—1630) had added the laws of motion. At about Locke's time Harvey (1578—1657) discovered the circulation of the blood, which considerably modified previous physiology. Boyle (1627—1691) discovered the atomic laws, which constituted the basis of modern chemistry, and which, as applied to natural processes, ruined much of the teaching of the Church. Newton (1642—1721) gave us the spectroscope, the planetary laws of motion, and the universal law of gravitation. Hutton (1726—1797) worked out a systematic foundation of geology (1795), which contradicted previous ideas of the creation and the age of the earth. Kant in 1757 and Laplace in 1796 formulated the nebular theory, with a similar result. Priestley (1733—1804) had many discoveries in gases to his credit, and in combination with Scheele discovered oxygen, which was finally established by Lavoisier (1743—1794). Cuvier (1769—1832) founded the science of comparative anatomy. Karl von Baer (1792—1876) discovered the mammalian ovum—the basis of comparative embryology, which, more than any other science, established man's relationship to the animal world. Wöhler (1802—1882) in 1828 dealt a great blow to religious belief by producing urea synthetically; this was thought to be a compound peculiar to animal life, and as such part of the handiwork of God. But probably the greatest blow of all was given by Darwin (1809—1882), who in 1859 published his theory of the " Origin of

Species." Of course one could enumerate examples at much greater length, but sufficient has been said to indicate the trend of thought that undermined belief in the supernatural.

The same scientific development had its influence also in philosophy, which we have seen reflected in the realism of the nineteenth century; but this realistic thought is itself undergoing a change consequent upon further scientific development. Most thinking in connection with the various sciences has long been freed from the supernatural, nevertheless until quite recently it stuck at trying to prove that mind is a mere product of ponderable matter. Later students are taking up the attitude that mind can never be material, that it indeed is not even physical, but that mind and matter are two different orders of being, running parallel to each other. The latter idea, which has received support from the electron theory, arises as a contradictory reflex from the idea that matter is nothing but materialised energy; so, they argue, if thought is energised matter then it should be measurable in terms of "work" done, just as are other forms of energy; and, since it is not measurable they conclude that it is not physical. Such a mode of reasoning, however, is a long way from proof, its weakness lying in the fact that, if it were true, nothing could be called physical until it had been measured; for example, the scent of a flower is admittedly physical, yet it cannot be said to be capable of measurement. It will be seen, therefore, that while these people are presumably scientific in their own fields of enquiry, they appear to be just as ignorant as many others when dealing with the problem of the mind, the obvious reason being that they employ the scientific method *in* their own special work, while outside that sphere they remain mere speculative wonderers. We shall see more of this in Part II. of our enquiry; for the present we must return to the sensational school of Bacon, Hobbes and Locke, and follow it in its migration to France.

France in the eighteenth century was in a state of feudalism, with, first, a superior territorial clergy;

second, the nobility; and third, the small landholders, who were striving to become what is now called the middle class (the serf or common labourer was " no class " at all). The small landholders were oppressed; there was economic servitude for the masses, combined with a corrupt State reeking with debauchery and general mental demoralisation. This was the field in which English materialism took root and registered its protest against the tyranny and corruption alike in morals, religion and State; in fact against all existing forms of authoritative restraint. The lower orders had lost all patience, for in addition to the corruption just mentioned, the new machinery being introduced from England was developing in the industrial areas a proletariat on the one hand and an industrial capitalist class on the other. In earlier times the Renaissance had been influential in producing a mental reaction against traditional thought, and in the period we are treating a development of that reaction was exemplified in the writings of men such as Rousseau and Voltaire; the rising movement also developed a school of materialist-atheists who, because they were engaged in producing a great Encyclopædia, came to be known as the Encyclopædists. Among these were several men of note—Diderot (the editor), D'Alembert, Montesqieu, Mirabeau and Baron D'Holbach, the last of whom, under the name of Mirabaud, wrote a work entitled " The System of Nature." This work is representative of French materialism; it attempts an explanation of the whole of nature, including man and his mind, on strictly mechanical lines. We may here see why Engels calls Bacon, Hobbes and Locke the fathers of eighteenth century materialists.

The argument running through " The System of Nature " starts from the assumption that everything that is, is natural, and is perpetually changing, the changes being due to motion. Therefore, everything in the universe is some combination or other of ponderable matter and motion. Mind is a product of so much brain matter, and takes effect according to the material constitution of any particular brain plus its subsequent experience. In addition to the motion of bodies, such as vehicles, the moving of a table, etc., which can be seen and which excites no particular attention, there is much motion that cannot be seen. What we call the Soul is really motion of the latter kind, but man not understanding it has presupposed a self-moving Soul of a supernatural order of being. There are no innate ideas, because the intellectual faculties depend upon sense perceptions, though thought itself being motion may be the object of thought, just as a given direction of motion may be changed by a force acting in a different direction.

Morality arises from the difference in the constitutions of different individuals. Since individuals vary according to their material or bodily constitution in addition to their experiences, and since each tries to get that which pleases him according to his constitution, there arises a diversity of interests. In the conflict of interests, *those individuals who have a knowledge of nature's laws and are therefore reasoning beings,* come to see that the greatest amount of good accrues to the individual only when the wishes of other individuals are taken into account; and so arise the laws of morals, the general love of man for man, justice in politics and law, etc.

Of course, such doctrines were opposed to tyrannical churches, governments and God. They constituted the rationalisation of the material interests of the middle class, and accordingly appeared as the consciously worked out mental stock-in-trade of the revolutionists of 1789, who, in place of the former morality of Church, State and feudal nobility, set up the moral standards of Liberty, Equality and Fraternity, based upon human reason. The laws underlying reason in the human mind were supposed to be eternal in the eternal matter and motion. With these one-sided materialists, matter was primary, while thought, being a mere product of brain substance plus experience, was secondary.

This teaching, though it does away with the Supreme mind of God as the source of morality, nevertheless remains very much at sea when trying to extract moral notions from the human mind, for after treating mind as an *effect* of matter, it elevates it to the *control* of matter by the fact that some men by the aid of their reason first find out the natural laws, which are deemed to be eternal, and then impose those laws on other men who, for lack of this knowledge, are deemed unreasonable. And, of course, "it stands to reason" that if natural laws are eternal, so will men who understand those laws be able to arrive at "eternally" correct systems of morality, politics, laws and truth. It all amounts to this, that they had elevated their own reason over that of their opponents, but did not know what to do with it when they had got it. They had scornfully cast on one side the transcendental speculations about the Supreme mind with its eternal moralities of Church and State, only in the end to develop motions of "eternal" love, freedom, equality, justice, etc., as a result of worshipping the human mind, and to this extent *they remained idealists,* though otherwise doing much good work on the philosophic materialist field. While Kant hailed the Revolution and freedom, he nevertheless, as stated in the last chapter, refuted these rationalist materialists on the philosophical field, thereby leaving room for faith in the supernatural, and thus safeguarding the basis of the authority of the middle class over the working class.

We have now to notice how materialism broke out in Germany in the nineteenth century; the story is much the same. With Austria's defeat by Napoleon at Austerlitz (1805) and Prussia's similar fate at Jena (1806), the dying embers of the Holy Roman Empire, whose flame had gone out at Constantinople in 1453, parted with their last curl of smoke. This resulted in a number of small German States acknowledging Napoleon as their protector. After the fall of Napoleon the princes of those States agreed to unite in a confederation, and in each State a *constitutional* government was to be set up; this was echoing the results of the French Revolution, for that nearly went too far on the side of the proletariat, so in Germany the middle class tried to get a voice in the government, without revolution. Prussia and Austria, however, were opposed to popular representation. The Prussian Government was oppressive and unjust from the standpoint of the middle class; it believed in its eternal rights and did not see why it should give its people a vote. We have seen that it found justification in Hegel's statement, "all that is reasonable is real, and all that is real is reasonable," and, accordingly, " what is, is what ought to be"; so Hegel was in favour with the Prussian Government, but this Government was not in favour with those people who wanted a voice in such public affairs as taxation, and who *did not believe* that the laws then existing were " what ought to be," consequently, since the Government persistently dilly-dallied with the question of popular representation, a revolution became necessary.

The whole affair, arising from the economic needs of the times, was, of course, political, but open opposition to the Prussian Government was dangerous work, so the prologue to the German revolution of 1848 (which found its immediate incentive in the French revolution of 1848), wherein the German middle class conquered "liberty," took the form of philosophical arguments in the press, which quite naturally criticised Hegel's idealism and the prevalent religion. At first the new philosophers fell back on French materialism in their fight against positive religion, which fight was also indirectly a political one, so it was not surprising that their philosophy contained the same *essential* glorification of the human mind after having dispensed with the Almighty one; this may be seen in the work of Ludwig Feuerbach (1804—1872, of Landshut, Erlanden and Bruckberg), who put human love as the guide in place of reason. Later ones, including Carl Vogt (1817—1895, of Giessen, German biologist), Jacob Moleschotte (1822—1893, Dutch physiologist, of Bois-le-Duc, settled in Italy), and Ludwig Büchner (1824—1899, of Darmstadt and Tübingen, physician), were more like the modern English rationalists of the Herbert Spencer type, and believed in nothing but matter and force; Haeckel (1834—1919, of Potsdam and Jena, biologist) even thought he had discovered the Soul cells. Though considerably more advanced from the standpoint of science, yet, from the standpoint of philosophy, the nineteenth century materialists (excepting those of the proletarian movement) were crude and mechanical, like those of the eighteenth century, in that ponderable matter was their base; so it is not necessary to work through their arguments, since they follow the same main lines and may be read in " Force and Matter "— an English translation (1864) of Büchner's " Kraft und Stoff " (1855).

At this point we must turn to the beginnings of proletarian science. The originators of proletarian social science (so called because it is not accepted by the university representatives of the capitalist class, but which, nevertheless, is nothing short of the science of society) sprang from Hegel's left wing, the " Young Hegelians." They were materialists, though in a different sense from those just treated. FEUERBACH, KARL MARX (1818—1883, of Treves, Cologne, Paris and London) and FRIEDRICH ENGELS (1820—1895, of Barmen, Paris, London and Manchester) were of this school; but Feuerbach belonged partly to the crude mechanicalists described by Engels as the " metaphysical materialists," because when they had finished with mechanical explanations they fell back on " pure " reason, though in Feuerbach's case it took the form of sentiment. If we remember that Hegel, though an idealist, was a dialectician, and that this was his chief contribution to philosophy, we shall see why Feuerbach, who broke through Hegel's " system " but retained the dialectic " method " of explaining all things as evolving out of other things, became a *materialist* dialectician. He believed that the evolution of society had in the past been along materialist lines, but he never could cut quite clear from the mechanical mode of thinking, and so, to escape the consequences, finally fell into the trap of an *eternal* human love as the directive force for the future. In this he was just like the other materialists, who prated of " pure " reason, that is, he was an idealist *with regard to the future.* Nevertheless, he did good work, and stands at the beginning of socialist philosophy; he is the *half way* house from Hegel's dialectic idealism to Marx and Engels' dialectic materialism, from which arises scientific socialism; Marx and Engels are accordingly the real pioneers in social science.

During the nineteenth century the work of Hegel gave increased momentum to the study of history, and Marx, one of the students, took the dialectic method from him, but applied it from the standpoint of materialism. Marx sought to show the law of social progress worked out in materialist dialectics, and one of his great discoveries was that history from early communism had been a series of struggles between different classes. From special studies of those struggles, plus the economic and social institutions of their periods, he arrived at his concept of "historical materialism," which is, that the economic mode of production (which means the way in which people get their living), determines the general form of society, and *the general mental attitude of any given period.*

It determines the kind of slavery, the kind of trade, the conflicting interests of different groups and their consequent political struggles. As a result of these struggles, the conquerers express their interests in various kinds of laws and of governments; meanwhile justifying themselves by claiming sanction from on High through different forms of religion and philosophy, while on the other hand those who are in opposition contend for an opposite view. Consequently, if the opposition should represent the economic interests of a rising class, it has necessarily to attack the existing political, legal, religious and philosophical institutions. This accounts for all rising movements being irreligious from the standpoint of those already in power, while developing a religion that serves their own purposes: it also accounts for the final rising movement, namely, that of the working class being non-religious. Literature also does but express the thought of its period, therefore, taken altogether, the political, legal, religious, philosophical and literary aspects of thinking, ultimately arise from and necessarily correspond to given modes of producing wealth; as the mode changes so does the thinking; and in the end the changes depend upon the evolution of tools or methods which enable wealth to be produced with a less expenditure of energy than formerly—*in this lies the essence of progress.* THE EVOLUTION OF SOCIETY EXPRESSES THE EVOLUTION OF TOOLS. This doctrine constitutes what is known as the "Materialistic Conception of History."

But the study of modes of production, apart from the purely technical side, expresses itself theoretically in the science of economics, wherein Marx discovered "the twofold nature of labour." This idea lies at the root of his theory of value. These generalisations could not have been discovered before, because a scientific theory of value necessarily concerns commodity production, and could not be thoroughly worked out until such production had reached an advanced stage, for not until the system of paying wages had separated more sharply the middle class from the working class, could it be clearly seen that the worker sells his labour power, that is, his strength or ability (physical and mental) *to perform* labour, but not the labour itself. Once the latter idea became clear the secret of the source of profit was out, and then a great many other things became clear. Marx' contributions to social science are the materialistic conception of history, and a well worked out theory of surplus value (profit in general).

After being exiled from the continent, Marx settled in England, where he had the chance of studying capital in its original home. In this work he was assisted by Engels, and between them they formulated the general proposition just outlined (Engels gives the greater part of the credit to Marx). They did this in the ordinary scientific manner, by first collecting historical material, forming a general opinion regarding it, deducing what ought to take place if their general opinion were correct, and finally noting the general agreement between their arguments and observed facts. By this method they arrived at their great generalisation which, though given at the end of the fourth chapter, will bear repeating—"In every historical epoch the prevailing mode of economic production and exchange, and the social organisation necessarily following from it, form the basis upon which is built up and from which alone can be explained the political and intellectual history of that epoch." But, though Marx and Engels supplied the general theory it remained for JOSEPH DIETZGEN (1828—1888, a working tanner born at Blankenberg) to work out the more detailed aspects of the mental reflex; this he did by showing the identity of mental work with the rest of nature. Dietzgen's work will be treated in Part II. of this book, so we leave it for the present, but before closing our historical survey, it may be advisable to refer to some curious products of bourgeois (middle class) idealism in relation to the misery of the proletariat (working class).

As the modern working class was evolved by capitalist development, and the resultant luxury on the one hand and misery on the other became more marked, there were not wanting "high souled" people to point out the "injustice" of such a state of things, and to suggest "remedies"; they thought it was only necessary to think of some scheme of betterment and then to apply it; these people are usually called utopians.

From early times there had been utopias (impracticable dreams of a better society) of different kinds, such as Plato's "Republic," Aristotle's "Politics,' the levelling tendencies of Christianity in the Roman Period with SS. Augustine, Basil and Benedict's "rules of life," including personal poverty, obedience to the laws of God, chastity, etc., and excluding any material considerations that would interfere with the contemplation of God; the whole pointing to a *community of interests.* Even in Feudal times there was a sort of community in land, there were landholders but not landowners; each landholder held of somebody higher in the social scale, and these ultimately of the King (or Church), who held it in trust for all his subjects. Through the Middle Ages there were communities of the monastic orders of Dominicans and Franciscans; the latter attacked not only the wealthy but even the

Pope on the question of the rights of private ownership of property. In 1381 John Ball, of Kent, quoting an earlier writer, asked "When Adam delved and Eve span, who was then the gentleman?"

But before this time these mediæval ideas of communism were being attacked, for Aquinas had begun in contradistinction to others of his order (Dominican) to defend private property; his teaching on this point may be summarised in the sentence: "A distinction of property is decidedly in accord with a peaceful social life." With him Nature makes no division of property, common property was sufficient before the Fall of man, but the Fall, and the consequent wickedness of man, introduced the supremacy of might, which makes the hope of peaceful intercourse to lie in agreement regarding division of property. Therefore, *in the interests of peace* (!) private property is justified, notwithstanding that "by nature all things are in common." Such teaching admits of either view, and both sides may quote him in support, but, in certain cases, he reserves the right of God, expressed through the Church or through the State, to decide either way. Here we have the *eternal* rights of the *Church,* ultimately from God.

In law, as distinct from religion, the ethics of property holding took a different turn and expressed themselves in antagonism to the supremacy of the Church. Feudal landholding, from the King downward, consisted of a series of contracts between man and man, and for the adjustment of grievances there existed the courts baron and customary, the sokes of privileged townships and the courts Christian (clerical criminal courts). There were quarrels between King, Barons and Church, for *power in law,* which ended in the King's favour. Here we have the supreme authority of the King as the *eternal right.* After this, came reform movements ending in constitutional governments based on the *eternal rights of the people* as being superior to either King or Church, so the *common* good *became divine,* but only to the extent of the middle class.

Then came the Industrial Revolution about 1760, with a new mode of production (the factory system), bringing with it a most shocking development of the already existing proletariat, and in the early nineteenth century there began modern Utopian Socialism both in France and in England, in which the *greater common good* was demanded in the name of the *eternal principles of humanity;* numerous " schemes " were propounded, and numerous sections of the working class are still playing the same game. In France, Saint-Simon thought that an aristocracy of ability should be the rulers; Fourier proposed the organisation of society into small communities each of four hundred families living on a square league of land; Louis Blanc worked for a State organisation of industry and Government workshops; Proudhon tried to introduce into political economy the *eternal* principles of " justice " and " liberty " by means of a fanciful arrangement of the method of exchange. In England it took the form of Chartism, based upon the *eternal* rights of the people. Robert Owen tried the experiment of industry run on communal lines, but when he attacked religion his socialism was called atheism. As opposed to this there arose an enthusiastic band of Christian socialists finding their inspiration in the Sermon on the Mount; they included Maurice, Kingsley and Ludlow. There was also the Anarchist school with ideas based on the *eternal* and immutable laws of nature, they therefore recognised no law of man over man, nor any God; among these may be mentioned Stirner, Bakunine, and, later, though in a small way, Paraf Javal, while Tolstoy was one of a different type, who denied the law of man but affirmed the law of God. Along with the above, Ruskin may be taken as typifying those who worship " the beautiful " as one means towards social regeneration.

On the industrial field the proletariat have organised in trade unions which again express an *abstract eternal* justice in the form of " a fair day's wage for a fair day's work "; while on the political field they have organised political parties who seek to apply " humanitarian " principles in government, or to effect humanitarian reforms in different aspects of social life.

It will be found that at the root of the activities of all the foregoing, whether they be Christian or anti-Christian, Theists or Atheists, *there exists an idealist philosophy* expressed in the first case as based upon the *eternal* truths of God, and in the second case upon the *eternal* principles of human love, or reason, from which arise eternal justice, eternal right, eternal freedom, equality and fraternity and many other eternal sentimentalities. They even go so far as claiming to be advanced in their thinking, while, as we shall see in Part II., their idealism is all along preventing them from seeing the limits to practicability.

In closing this Introduction to the History of Thinking, if we may dignify such a small and rough work with that title, we may remember the evolution of brains, the production of religion and mythology through ignorance of nature; that the Ionian philosophers turned to nature and found nothing but change; later ones turned to examine thinking and threw nature on one side, thus casting out just the material needed, although as yet it was too early in the economic development of the world to solve such a problem. They thought they had discovered the permanent principle in mind, but their own logic reduced their systems to scepticism and faith. Faith lived on for many centuries with philosophy as a kitchen help until a revival of logic led the said kitchen help to demand more and more days " off," and finally to give a couple of centuries' notice of leaving. Philosophy ultimately freed itself from theology or nearly so, but by that time a new method of investigating all sorts of questions had sprung up, the inductive, or scientific method, that brought in its train a positive science which likewise freed itself from philosophy. In science, men are agreed as to the accuracy of the laws discovered *after they have passed the experimental stage*, and by means of those laws can predict results (though it must be remembered that changing conditions bring new laws). But, notwithstanding the successes of science in fields other than mental, philosophy imagined thought was produced by pure reason, though no two philosophers could ever agree, and they have remained in that unscientific state to this day. Meanwhile, Kant turned his attention to examining reason. From his time materialism and idealism became more decidedly separated but ultimately got reconciled by Dietzgen, though towards the end of the nineteenth century the cry " Back to Kant ' had been raised as a safety valve against the rising materialism. Dietzgen, for the first time in the history of the world, made thinking into a science, and consequently philosophy, as such, comes to an end except for some mystic rags with which a few grown-up children love to play.

The new materialism of the Marxian brand is rapidly influencing both the political and industrial wings of the working class movement. The capitalist class, in mortal dread at losing its grip of "eternal" realities, no longer cries " Back to Kant," if it *must* recognise a doctrine of change, then, hurry along to Bergson, the mystic, whose only reality is a changing "time." The workers will not be held down by religion; patriotism is no longer a trustworthy tag, its gorgeous exterior having become somewhat tarnished through the war; so, if our masters, as represented in their university teachers, could only get us mystified with Bergson, their " great man theory," namely, that social progress is due to the thinking of the " great " men, would, they think, receive another lease of life.

While the practical fight lies between the forcefully-defended rights of private property on the one hand, and the forceful abolition of slavery on the other, the theoretical fight lies between the remains of philosophy, a false economics and a so-called impartial history on the capitalists' side, as against a scientific method of thinking, a science of economics and a history alive with class struggles on the workers' side. We now leave the history of thinking and pass to a short exposition of its science.

PART II

LOGIC, OR THE SCIENCE OF UNDERSTANDING

PART II

LOGIC, OR THE SCIENCE OF UNDERSTANDING

CHAPTER IX

Logic applied to the General Nature of Thought (Mind) and of Things (Matter)

From the time when the Greeks turned away from nature and took to examining mind, down to the present, there have been two main streams of philosophic thought which in their passage have not always been clear and distinct from each other, nor has even their general nature been interpreted in the same way at all times; these lines of thought are idealism and materialism. After Descartes they became more clearly distinguished, and still more so after Kant.

Both materialists and idealists take existence as a fact; the materialist (old school) says the nature of this existence is ponderable matter (the later ones, such as Sir Oliver Lodge, have etherialised it but still regard it as physical), though he does not deny the phenomena of mind; he conceives of it as some sort of emanation from matter, but which has no existence in its own right. On the other hand, the idealist says the nature of existence is mental, though he does not deny the phenomena of matter, but conceives of it as an illusion of mind. It will be seen that each admits the phenomena of the other and tries to interpret it in terms of his own particular fancy; each can prove to his own satisfaction that the other is wrong, though each fails to prove to his opponent's satisfaction that he himself is right.

Now it must be remembered that the terms "mind" and "matter" are merely names which enable us to distinguish between two different things, but, since the names are not the things, it does not follow that because we use two names there are two *completely* separate and distinct things, so different that they have *nothing* in common, the two may be just two parts of one thing and only mentally separated. As we go on we shall see that all the philosophic word-spinning arises from the use of a rigid logic which first makes mental distinctions, gives names to the parts, and then *treats the parts as being distinct and separate,* whereas in reality they are not so; it was in this way that the old philosophers first started with unity (the universe) and then instinctively separated it into mind and matter without being fully conscious of what they had done, since when their philosophic descendants have been staring at mind in one hand and matter in the other, wondering which part constitutes both parts.

Before passing on to study the newer logic, which treats of thinking in relation to a constantly-changing universe, it may be as well to give some of the general laws of this rigid logic for purposes of comparison. First, there is the law of identity, by which we say A is A; second, the law of contradiction which says that A is not B; and third, the law of the excluded third which says that A is not part of B. According to the first of these rules, a thing is what it is; according to the second, no thing is what it is not; and, according to the third, no thing is part of what it is not. As examples:—

A square is a square, a square is not a circle, nor is a square part of a circle.

A straight line is straight, it is not crooked, nor is it partly crooked.

A moving thing is in motion, it is not still, nor is it partly still.

Land is land, land is not water, nor is it partly water.

A door that is shut is shut, it is not open, nor is it partly open.

In our everyday business we all employ this sort of

logic, nor could we manage very well without it, nevertheless it needs supplementing by the dialectic method which shows that all things are constantly flowing into other things, and consequently that all fixed statements, such as the foregoing, can be true only within certain well-defined limits, and are never wholly true; and which shows, furthermore, that unless the limits of a question are clearly defined, *no statement regarding it can have any meaning,* because no relationship between the implied fact and the statement has been established; this, in working class language, means " let us know what we are talking about, otherwise talking is no good." As an example, take the statement " a door that is open is not shut "; while this looks like commonsense, in reality it is not sense at all unless we state the purpose in view, for, assuming a door to be open one inch, it would be open for the purpose of letting in noise or a draught, but it would not be open for allowing a person to pass, so accordingly the truth of the statement will vary as the purpose to be realised varies. As another example, suppose it be said that " right is right, right cannot be wrong," this statement has no meaning at all unless we connect it with some definite purpose, when we very quickly discover that any particular statement might be right in relation to some purpose but wrong in relation to others.

Logic, it need hardly be said, is to enable us to make distinctions between different things so that we may find our way about in the mental world without making mistakes. But to be any good, the work of distinguishing must obviously start from some point about which nobody can quarrel, something that is certain; and the rock-bottom fact from which nobody can get away is plainly that of existence, for it is clearly impossible to argue about that which does not exist, and since " existence " includes everything, existence, here, means the same thing that we call Universe, or Being or Nature. People who think of a Creator outside the universe are attempting to imagine a universe that is not a universe. So the universe exists, *and is the only thing that exists.* Consequently, the thing we call mind must be a part of it, and the thing we call matter must be another part of it, they differ, of course, otherwise we should not require a different name for each; and since mind or understanding is busily engaged in understanding both itself and as much of the remainder as it can get at, there is evidently a relation between the understanding which knows and the object that is known, even when the understanding is concerned with itself. Our present work is to study this relationship, to trace out its connections and limitations, and our starting point is the whole universe, the only single thing, the only absolutely true unit.

A unit is, of course, capable of being divided into an infinite number of parts after the manner represented in Fig. 2, which shows that while one-sixteenth is not another sixteenth yet they are both parts of one-eighth, two-eights are parts of one-quarter, and similarly with all the rest.

Fig. 2. The Universe.

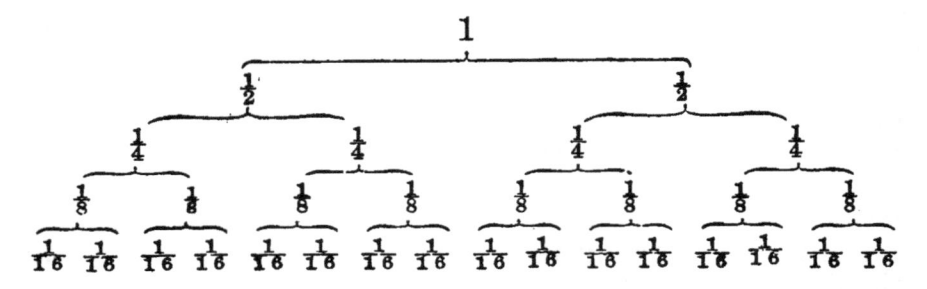

$$1 = \underbrace{\tfrac{1}{2} + \tfrac{1}{2}}_{} = \underbrace{\tfrac{1}{4}+\tfrac{1}{4}+\tfrac{1}{4}+\tfrac{1}{4}}_{} = \underbrace{\tfrac{1}{8}+\cdots+\tfrac{1}{8}}_{8} = \underbrace{\tfrac{1}{16}+\cdots+\tfrac{1}{16}}_{16}$$

For certain purposes, any of these fractional parts may be taken as a unit; for example, an eighth, when considered as a unit, may be split into two halves (not sixteenths), but we must never forget that this is merely a mental convenience because the only *real* unit is the universe. Therefore, we may start anywhere, call our particular point a unit and break it down into its parts, or we may take a given number of parts and with them construct a unit. The contradiction that exists when we say that one half is not the other half (A is not B) is reconciled as soon as we consider them joined together in one unit; the *idea of contradiction* is, therefore, a product of our understanding which is constantly either splitting up units or constructing them in classifying the different parts of the universe.

Now this is very easy to see when put in the form of figures, and although the essential character of understanding is number, yet, when we come to apply it to the universe or to any part of it, the idea is so strange that most folks never realise that it is what human brains are doing all along, and through the lack of a knowledge of this general principle of thinking they necessarily perform their thinking instinctively instead of scientifically, and consequently make far more mistakes than they would if they knew the scientific principle and consciously applied it.

To understand the universe the understanding divides it into a great number of parts, that is, it classifies or separates the parts *and gives them names* to distinguish one from the other, though in reality these parts do not exist separately; for example, the universe, though it is in itself one whole, may be divided mentally into solar systems, a solar system may be divided into a central sun and several planets of which the earth is one, and the earth may be divided into land and water, and so on to infinity. For ordinary purposes it would be false to say that land and water are the same thing, it would be a contradiction; nevertheless, this contradiction, which is a product of the understanding, disappears if we say that land and water are both parts of the earth, for if one is a part of the earth and the other equally so, then, *considered as parts of the earth*, each is the same as the other. From this it follows that a thing can be the same as another thing and at the same time be different from it, and all this depends upon the way we look at any given problem, in other words, depends upon the purpose we have in view; whereas old-style logic would say " land is land, land is not water, nor does it partake of the nature of water in any way," and, therefore, that " land is not water " is a true statement—true for all time; though in the next argument it might seek to prove that England is the best of all *lands*, forgetting that England contains many lakes, rivers, reservoirs, etc.

Very well, let us with the help of the newer logic turn to the question of mind and matter! The idealist insists on mind as the dominant reality, the old materialist looks at the question the other way about and pins his faith to ponderable matter. Contrary to each of these schools, we start from the existence of a real universe which our understanding may divide in hundreds of ways according to its particular problem at any given moment, and since our problem just now is that of the understanding itself, then *for the purposes of this discussion* we divide the universe into mind and matter, or, to be more correct, thought and things.

But what shall we call the universe itself? Is it a material or physical or real universe? Well, it is certainly a real universe, for we cannot deny that even thought is real thought; thought is not nothing at all, consequently thought, being part of the universe, it must possess the same universal nature as is possessed by everything else, whatever that should be. "But," the reader may say, "thought is so different from a lump of coal, surely it is not suggested that they have the same nature"? "And," one might ask in return, "are not wireless radiations different from coal and yet both are described as physical"? "True enough, but still, thought is different even from 'wireless,' thought has an intellectual character that no other thing has." "Just so; but if every other thing had the same character there would be no object in making the distinction; it is precisely because thought has a special character of its own, we give it a special name." We give wireless radiations their special name to distinguish them from coal and all other things. A brain is different from wireless instruments or our legs, so why should we be surprised because all these things exhibit different functions? It is not marvellous that brains should think, but it would be exceedingly so if they did not. We do not walk on our brains and think with our legs. The peculiar function of brains is to think, of legs to walk, and of wireless instruments to transmit and receive electrical radiations, so why should we expect anything different, or why should we single out thought (called mind) as having a nature so special and peculiar as to separate it *entirely* from all the rest of the universe? Thinking is the function of a physical brain, just like walking is a function of physical legs, and even though the conversion of sense stimuli into thought is not understood, this does not prove that thought is not physical, if it did, then, by comparison, we should have to say that electricity is not physical because we do not understand the nature of the conversion of magnetism into electricity. Even so, does it follow that if " wireless " and thought are physical that they are also material? Well, that depends upon how the reader mentally divides the universe. If he divides it into the ponderable, such as coal, iron, pencils, etc., and the imponderable, such as thought, light, sound, electricity, ether or gravity, and then decides to describe the ponderable as material and the imponderable as immaterial, that is his own affair, but please let him remember he did it himself, it is not so in nature merely because he arranged his classification that way, and to describe thought as psychical does not alter its nature. Had we all along been in the habit of calling *all* things material the present question would not have arisen. So, if we call thought material it is in order to bring its description (its nature is already in line) into line with that of the rest of what most people, ourselves included, call the material universe; and the term "material" is as good as any we can find, for old-style logic made its distinction between mind and matter but left us without a term that would include both; therefore, in discussing the relation that exists between the different parts of the universe we must bear in mind that thought is a material part just like any other.

Having seen that the universe can be mentally divided into an infinite number of parts, as suggested in Fig. 3. all of which have their special natures and special names to distinguish them from one another, in addition to their general material nature and corresponding name, our progress will consist in noting how these different parts are related to each other. All parts enter into relations with other parts, though each part, excepting thought, has *a limited range* of relationships which

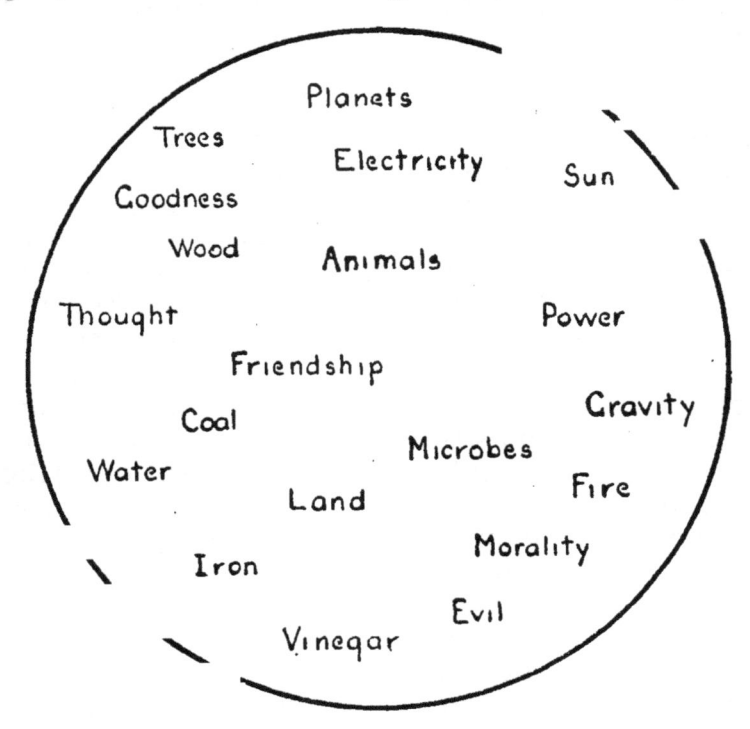

Fig. 3. Parts of Material Universe.

depends upon its particular constitution; thought alone is capable of entering into relation with *every* other part. Take, for example, vinegar and iron. If we pour vinegar on iron it dissolves the iron and forms rust, but this rust is due as much to the iron as to the vinegar, therefore, to say that vinegar is a solvent is wrong if considered by itself, because vinegar is not a solvent *unless taken in relation* to something that dissolves by contact with it. Or, to say that vinegar is an acid is wrong, it is an acid when in contact with somebody's tongue but not in those relationships where acidity is not produced. If we say that water is liquid, we mean it is liquid in relation to certain temperatures; at other temperatures it becomes ice or steam, its liquid state is, therefore, the product of itself *taken in conjunction with some other part or parts of the universe*, such as heat or gravity. From these examples we see that no one thing is anything at all by itself, any one part of the universe is what it is only because of its relation with something else, therefore every so-called " single " thing is a product of many things, it is a mental unit made up of fractions; for example, a piece of iron cannot be conceived without its shape, weight, colour, heat, etc., once change the relationships and the thing changes, and when it has changed so much that its previous *general* nature is changed it requires a different name. As an instance, imagine the *general* character of dust along a road; after very light rain we should say the dust was laid; the nature of the dust would be changed, though, *not so much as to make it require another name*, for we should still call it dust, but after heavy rain its nature would be changed to such an extent that it would have acquired a different *general* character and we should have to describe it as mud. Giving names, however, presupposes that we have thought about something, in fact, we cannot imagine anything existing that has not been thought about, for in the very act of attempting to do so we are already thinking about it, so this brings us to consider the relation between thought and everything with which it comes into contact.

Thought—Its General Character. A thought like any other part of existence, *is made up of many parts.* It arises from the relation between a thinking brain (and a brain that does not think loses its character and ceases to be what we mean when we speak of a brain) and some object about which the brain thinks. This thought, just like the rust, is as much a product of the object as of the thinking, for it is clear there never was a brain that could think about nothing. And again, it will be clear that there must be some medium by which the relation between brain and object is established. This medium is composed of our five senses (and possibly a sixth in the course of being evolved)—seeing, hearing, smelling, feeling and tasting.

These senses acquaint us with the various parts of objects, for any single object, as already stated, is made up of many parts, such as shape, weight, colour, heat, etc. Take, for illustration, an apple; our sense of sight perceives its roundness and colour, when we chew it our sense of hearing perceives a sound, it gives off a characteristic odour perceived by our sense of smell, by our sense of touch or feeling we perceive that it has weight, shape, solidity, coolness, etc., and our sense of taste acquaints us with its specific flavour. Not one of these sense perceptions is sufficient by itself, nor, indeed, would they all, taken together, give us a mind picture of the apple, without a brain which, so to speak, adds them together. The peculiar function of the brain is to combine or to generalise all these sense perceptions *into one idea* to which it gives the name " apple " for the purpose of distinguishing that particular combination of parts from other and different combinations. If we had another sense capable of being applied we should get our idea extended accordingly, just as in the reverse case our idea would be narrowed, as, for example, in the case of a blind person who has no sense of colour; from this it will be seen that a brain cannot replace any of the senses, brain and senses having each their special functions to perform. It is important also to remember that although thinking and thought occur at the same time, they are not the same things. Thought is a *result*, thinking is the *work of producing* that result, thinking, however, is impossible without some *object* to think about, so the whole thing is a sort of trinity that might be represented by a triangle as in Fig. 4.

Since it is the peculiar function of the brain to generalise sense perceptions into ideas, and since our ideas constitute knowledge, it will be clear that understanding consists solely of our ability to combine different parts of the universe under one head or name, whereby we may know it from something else; or, speaking in terms of number, our ability to combine four-sixteenths into one-quarter, two-eighths into a quarter, and so on; or, again, to use a more practical illustration, we may take apples, oranges and bananas,

THINKING

etc., and give them the general name of fruit; add to these, vegetables, bread, meat, drinks, etc., our extended generalisation becomes food; add, again,

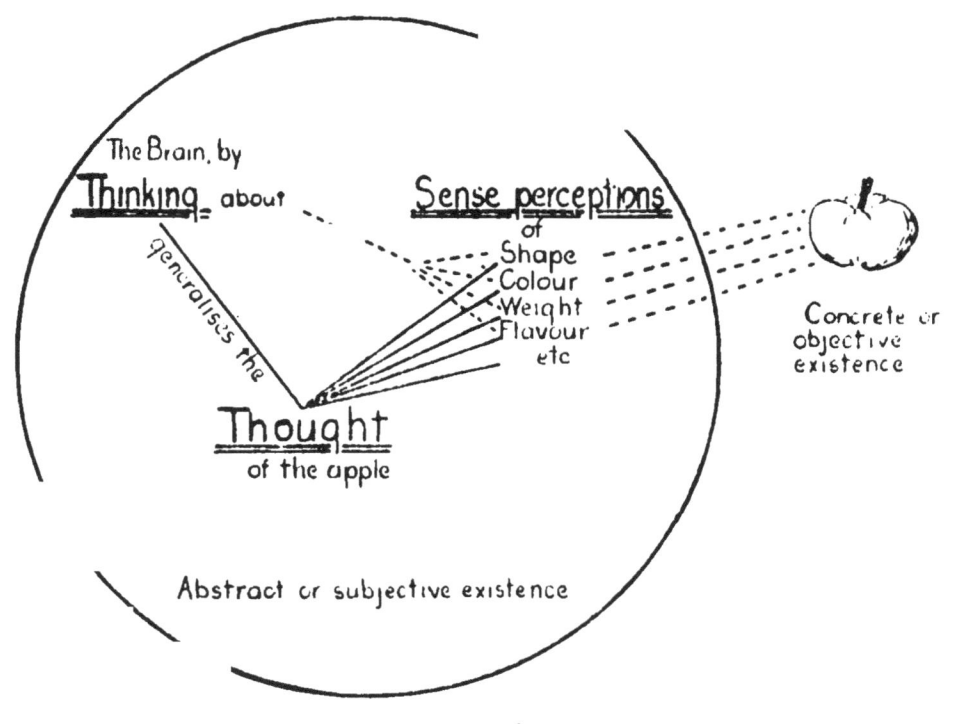

Fig. 4. Brain Work.

clothes, fuel, furniture, books, houses, we might call these, altogether, the necessaries of life. No matter how large or how small, every single idea is made up of parts; even the idea of an atom contains parts such as shape, weight, chemical peculiarity, size, etc.

It is possible to mentally generalise or combine any number of parts up to the limit of the whole universe, whether they are actually combined in that way or not outside the head, as, for example, when an artist conceives a fanciful picture, or a novelist writes an extravagant novel, or when, as in a nightmare, the Devil with cloven hoofs and a red-hot pitchfork carried us off to Hell, or when we imagine a Government that acts impartially to everybody, or when somebody tells the workers that "a better spirit" between masters and men will solve economic troubles to all peoples' satisfaction. It must be borne in mind that these fancies are all truly parts of the universe, that is, they are real fancies, even mistakes and lies are real mistakes and true lies; we mean by this that they have a real existence, for thought, as we have said, is real; it would be a funny contradiction to speak of "imaginary" thought. What, then, is the difference between truth and error? This question brings us to consider the other part of brain activity.

We have hitherto considered the brain as a generalising instrument, wherein it combines sense perceptions into an abstract idea or unit. But it also works the other way; it analyses an idea by breaking it down into its parts. We have seen that every single idea is composed of parts which by division run to infinity, and which by addition run into one another up to the limit of the universe; this for us is also infinity. We have further seen that no idea is possible without both a brain and some object, connected by the senses. Now where the idea or abstract picture in the mind corresponds with some object outside the mind (any part of existence whatsoever, including thought, may be the object of thought), it will be clear that such a picture will be a true picture, but if the opposite is the case it will be false. By way of illustration, suppose a novelist wrote a tale describing a foreign tribe of human beings who lived by eating coal; this tale would be a true tale in so far as it itself exists as a tale, but it would be false in so far as coal *outside the mind* is not a food, and, therefore, to generalise coal under the name of food would be an error because it would lack that correspondence between abstract mind picture and outside objective existence which is necessary for truth; it would be like trying to make three-sixteenths into one-eight. Truth, then, evidently consists of those mental or subjective generalisations which correspond with objective reality, and just as objective reality changes, so does truth change; for example, we have just said that coal is not a food, but suppose that in the future some chemist discovered a way of cooking coal so that it could be eaten, and the energy which is now latent in it be assimilated by the human body, such changed conditions would bring it about that what is now error would then be true, and our unit (food) would be enlarged to accommodate the new factor. Therefore, since all ideas are built up as mind pictures from sense perceptions of material objects, tangible and intangible, to test an idea for truth, we must break it down into its parts, then look outside the mind to see if the previous mental combination is possible as an outside objective combination; if it is, the idea is true; if not, it is untrue. By now it should almost go without saying that such generalisations as sea serpents, mermaids, two-headed donkeys, angels, and happy hunting grounds, in fact, all the ghosts of heaven and earth, holy and unholy, are those whose parts are abstract mind pictures taken from concrete parts of nature outside the mind and added together *inside* the mind; although *the parts* exist outside the mind, *the combination does not,* consequently they are errors, for the reason that *too many factors* have been combined to agree with objective reality.

Still, the matter is not ended, for even though we confine our attention to real objective combinations, another difficulty arises, because *if all things run into one another* how shall we know when a mind picture corresponds with reality, where shall we look, where shall we start with our generalising, or where shall we stop? There is only one thing possible, and that is to select or mentally *mark off that part of the universe the truth of which is to be sought* ("let us know what we are talking about"), *and then abstract its general character.* Our selected number of parts we may imagine to thin out at each end where the general character is merging or flowing into other things with different names; these thin ends are the special parts, as compared with the general body, and if we speak of them as being typical of the general body, we should be wrong, we should be taking *too few factors* to agree with the general objective reality; consequently these special parts must be ignored, they do not constitute the truth concerning *that particular number of parts* because they do not express its general character, so truth is, accordingly, that which is general within a clearly defined part of existence; this is true logic, because it provides for a continual readjustment of our abstract mind pictures, to correspond with a continually changing objective reality. As a simple example it would be true to describe apples and bananas as fruit, but false to describe them simply as food without any qualification, notwithstanding that fruit is a food; this would be false for the simple reason that the term " food " denotes something having a *general* nature possessed by many other things as well as fruit, so to say that fruit constitutes food would be making the special element into the general. Again, food is not the necessaries of life, it is only one of them; the " necessaries of life " constitutes a wider unit or generalisation, because its common or general nature is possessed by other things as well as food. *Truth, then, is any statement that accurately expresses the general or common features of a certain definite number of parts and, of course, is relative to those parts, vary the number of parts and the common nature will vary, and truth likewise.*

Though this logic is easy in theory, it is not always easy in practice, so from this point onwards we will apply it to a series of questions by way of illustration, remembering that *no* idea is possible without sense perception, and therefore every idea may be understood by tracing it to its sense perceived source.

Mind. The brain, of course, is not the mind, it is the seat of the mind; but since the word " mind " certainly stands for an idea of something, there arises the question, what is this " something," " or what is the mind itself ? Let us apply our logic. Since every single idea is built up of parts, and is expressed by a name, if we analyse the idea represented by its name we shall get at *the nature of the thing* for which the name stands, therefore, to understand the mind, we must examine its parts. When we speak of mental work we think of a vast number of ideas, memories, reflections, judgments, acts of the will, etc., in short, our general reasoning. And we think of the mind as a being of some shadowy kind that performs all the reasoning. However, if we break down the idea of mind into its parts, we find that memories are ideas, reflections are ideas, judgments are ideas, in fact, all our reasoning is composed of ideas, the mind, then, consists of a bundle of ideas which are, as we know, produced by sense perceptions (the stimulus of which may last quite a time, as in the case of memory) being generalised by our brains, so there can be no " reason " or " mind " that produces or originates ideas without something to think about, without sense perceptions. Looked at like this it becomes clear that what we call " mind " is not a shadowy something that we can never get at and which thinks thoughts entirely unaided, but on the contrary it is the sum total of all the ideas we possess, and apart from these ideas there is nothing at all, for even the idea of " mind " must have a basis of sense perceptions; it is simply that the brain combines all its ideas into one generalisation, that is, into one unit to which it gives the name of " mind "; so mind, then, is nothing but generalised thought. No wonder scientists cannot find it with the knife and the microscope; theologians, of course, are interested in not looking for it.

Still, there is one point that needs explaining; if ideas are impossible *without sense perceptions,* how does the brain get the idea of mind, seeing that the mind is composed of ideas inside the head? Which of our senses enables us to become aware of them? It is the sense of feeling, for when we are thinking, *we feel that we are thinking*, a fact which everyone may test; for example, we feel sorry, or glad, or we feel we could hit certain people at times. In this case the sense of feeling presents a series of perceptions of thoughts to the brain, and the brain in its functioning generalises them into the one idea of " mind." Our logic thus solves the twenty-six-centuries-old problem of " mind " and " pure reason"; let us next see what it can do with the corresponding problem of matter or things.

Matter—Its General Nature. What is matter? Let us apply our logic in just the same way as when examining mind. If every idea is built up of parts, we ask what are the parts constituting the idea of matter? Take for example a table. Kant would tell us that all we know about the table is composed of its appearances, but that in addition there must be *something behind the appearances*, though we never can know it, a "thing in itself." Various philosopher-scientists say the same thing in various ways; for instance, that light is not the beautiful colour we see, but an ethereal wave motion of which we become aware by noting its effects; or, that the colour of an object, or its weight, shape, etc., are only attributes of the object and not the thing in reality. They tell us that not a particle of matter is ever destroyed, that its form is constantly changing, but, through all the changes of form *the essential matter remains*. Now, what is this essential matter when divested of its attributes? Some say we shall never know, for nothing ever appears to our senses but the attributes, and these do not constitute the essence, for the essence or true nature of matter is something that lies beyond.

It is indeed perfectly true that our senses do not acquaint us with its true nature, but our understanding (brain function) does, and when scientists say we shall never know, it can only be because they do not understand how all understanding takes place. The true or essential nature of matter does not, as we have said, appear to the senses but to our understanding, though the parts of the idea come to us through the senses just like the parts of all ideas. Imagine for a moment what would become of the table if we took away one after the other all its attributes. When we have taken away its colour, solidity, weight, shape, hardness, grain, etc., there is nothing left, nothing at all; it therefore *could not appear to our senses*, and yet we have the idea of it;

now how can we have the idea of a thing that does not exist?

The brain first thinks of all kinds of objects—water, horses, coal, etc., etc.; these objects have each the *common* attribute of being material, even though they each possess many different and *special* attributes (also material); the brain, then, separates the special characteristics from the general, and with these many parts of *material generality,* constructs the idea of " essential matter " as distinct from its attributes. So, only in the light of our logic does it become clear to us that matter, *apart* from its attributes, is nothing but an abstract generalisation. Therefore, in reality, matter consists of the sum total of its attributes, its general nature is unceasing change, and there is nothing else beyond. We see, then, that this " essential matter " is a creature of the mind; this concept may perhaps be rendered more easily intelligible if we think for a moment of the impossibility of there being any stable unchanging matter *apart* from its changing forms, without any attributes, without any form. The raw material of material attributes is as funny as imaginary thought!

It will now be clear that mind is not a " thing in itself " independent of thoughts, and which thinks thoughts or produces them out of its inmost recesses; in reality, it is the brain which generalises sense perceptions into ideas, and these ideas, taken altogether, constitute the mind. It will also be clear that matter is not a " thing in itself " independent of its forms, and which takes first one form, then another; it is the brain which generalises selected sense perceptions of material attributes into the idea of matter, so that in reality all attributes taken together constitute matter. So mind consists of the sum total of thoughts, and matter consists of the sum total of its forms; consequently mind and matter *considered as separate entities* (things existing by themselves) are nothing but mental generalisations, produced instinctively, but, because the understanding did not understand itself, it did not know how it got them and thought they represented definite parts of objective reality.

CHAPTER X

Logic applied to Physical Science

In the last chapter we were occupied in explaining the principles of that logic which treats the universe as a thing in motion, in opposition to ordinary logic which makes its distinctions and considers them as stationary. In our treatment we dealt with the general nature of thought and of things, and we saw that both thought and things were material or physical, so that science in any line of enquiry must of necessity be physical science; nevertheless, as all divisions of the universe are made by the understanding in its desire for classification, we now, *for the purposes of this chapter,* take the liberty of dividing all science into the mental and the physical; we therefore use the word "physical" in the sense usually attached to it as meaning all that is not mental or *meta*physical; consequently we shall be concerned with such things as force, light, sound, matter, cause, effect, and so on. Since the basis of the solution of every problem, so far as logic is concerned, lies in understanding the origin of all the ideas contained in it, our progress will consist in applying to such things the principles we have already learned. It is futile to say that it does not matter where we get the ideas so long as we have them, for the reason that so long as we cannot trace them to their source we cannot make any scientific selection, nor can we understand how understanding itself takes place.

Nature. Take first the idea of nature, since it is the basis of all science. What is Nature?
Remembering that every single idea is produced by

the brain generalising a number of sense perceptions, and thus reducing them to unity, we must attack the idea of Nature by breaking it into its parts to see where we get it.

Nature consists of the sum total of all the things we experience with the aid of our senses; all these things have their special natures according to their constitution, but the understanding puts these specialities on one side, it mentally takes the general natures of all things apart from their special characters, and combines them into one abstract whole, to which it gives the name of Nature, which afterwards is supposed to be the parent of the specialities. Therefore it is not our senses that perceive " Nature," they only perceive the various parts separately, but with those parts the understanding constructs the idea of nature *in general;* it is accordingly the understanding which perceives nature as a whole. As a rule, when we speak of Nature producing beautiful flowers, healing wounds, causing this and that, or when, as is quite usual, we speak of " the wonders of Nature " after the manner of poets and dreamers, including not a few scientists, who are continually marvelling about our great "mother nature," we have a vague, indistinct notion of Nature being something unknowable, a kind of universal directive agency which somehow, in a transcendental manner, causes all the things we experience; but with our logic we see that there is no " mother nature " apart from all the things that go to construct her; so this idea is just an instance of the understanding constructing one thing out of many parts, or, as it is often put, constructing unity out of multiplicity.

According to this *all* things are natural, and cannot be anything else; so what do we mean when we say a thing is unnatural, has the term no meaning? Oh yes. We do not mean the thing has no nature at all. It means the unusual, or special, that which is not general, or that to which we are not accustomed, and which, therefore, is not included in our *general* conception of what we expect. So the natural and the unnatural are simply two mental divisions of those things we have experienced, the one general, the other special. For example, it is not usual for people in England to murder their parents when they are getting old, and if somebody did we should probably say it was a most unnatural thing to do; it is, of course, unusual or special. But if it were generally practised, as it was among low savage hunting tribes, it would be regarded as quite all right and the most natural thing to do. To give another example: when exceptionally dark clouds come overhead during the daytime, that give the appearance of night, it is said to be unnatural. We therefore see the unnatural to be merely the *general character of the unusual or special,* whereas the natural is the *general character of that which is usual,* and therefore *more widely general.*

Old style logic would say, the natural is natural, it is not unnatural, nor is it partly unnatural. Dialectic logic says that the unnatural is both unnatural and natural at one and the same time, for the reason that all things are natural, though we only give the name natural to that which is general in relation to any particular part of nature which happens to be under discussion, while the unnatural is any special circumstances relating to that same part. If Nature in its entirety is being discussed, then there can be nothing unnatural, for nature in that sense includes everything. We turn now to consider some special parts of nature.

Cause and Effect. There is a fourth rule of logic known as "the law of adequate cause," which means that every effect must have a sufficient cause; and it is quite commonly accepted by "educated" people who are ignorant of logic (true logic) that not only must an effect have a cause, but that this cause must be the effect of a previous cause which is the effect of a still more previous cause, and so on back to the "first cause," which itself never was caused. Some say the first cause is God, others Nature, though all believe its essential character to be unknown; and no wonder, when we consider for a moment that if an effect had never taken place the cause could never have been a cause, therefore the effect is as much the cause of the cause being a cause, as the cause is the cause of the effect—if the child had never been born the father would never have been its father, so the child is as much the cause of the father being the father, as the father is the cause of the child. But what really constitutes a cause? Let us apply our logic and break the ideas of cause and effect into their parts, thus seeing where we get them.

With the understanding that all parts of the universe are continually changing, it is obvious that some of the parts precede others in the order of time. The senses supply the brain with sense perceptions of those parts that *generally* precede, and the understanding adds them together to form the idea of cause. For example, in summer, showers of rain *generally precede* or bring about a cooler atmosphere; the senses of sight and of feeling supply the brain with perceptions of falling rain preceding a feeling of coolness at such times, whereupon the brain function combines all those separate perceptions into the one idea of rain being the cause of the coolness. In the same way the idea of effect may be broken into its parts; they consist of sense perceptions of phenomena that *generally follow*. For example, the sense of feeling supplies the brain with perceptions of coolness that generally follow the falling of rain at such times, and the brain function combines these perceptions into the one idea of coolness being the effect of the rain.

But looking a little more closely, we see that rain could not cause coolness were there no heat for it to absorb, so the heat is as much a cause of coolness as the rain. And again, if the coolness had not taken place after the rain (and there are times when it does not, as far as our senses tell us) the rain could not have been a cause, therefore, at the time when it did take place the coolness is as much a cause of the rain causing coolness as the rain itself. From this we see there is no such thing as a cause " in itself." It is the understanding that constructs the ideas of cause and effect. And, moreover, with every extension of parts so does the cause vary; for example, if rain is the cause of coolness, so is the heat of the atmosphere, and the contour of the land that produces rain, also the wind that carries the moisture, and the sun that raised it. Here we see that all these small generalisations constitute the special or particular parts out of which the understanding constructs the greater generalisation of a "first cause"; and then, because man cannot understand a cause not consciously directed, and this is because his knowledge of the universe takes the form of intelligence, he says there must be a God who causes it all; but, when we remember that *all ideas,* including that of cause, are abstract mental generalisations of sense perceptions, it becomes a waste of time to think about a first cause that is *independent* of a material basis, for it is obvious there cannot be any such thing. The idea is a wrong generalisation of parts that have no corresponding generalisation in reality. Nature as the great uncaused cause, *consists of the sum total of all the smaller or special causes,* so there is no *one* cause except as a mental abstraction.

Absolute Straightness. It is well known that the most perfect line, drawn by the most able of draughtsmen, with the aid of the best instruments and on the best paper for the purpose, will, if seen through a miscroscope, show many irregularities. We may, therefore, conclude there is no absolute straightness in nature, and yet the idea of it plays a very important part in geometry, mechanics, architecture, etc. Now, if every idea is based on sense perceptions, and if there is no absolute straightness in nature for the senses to perceive, how do we come by the idea? To solve this question we must follow our logic and break the idea into its parts. In nature there are many lines that appear to be straight, some more so than others, so the brain takes the many sense perceptions of objects, separates the qualities of straightness from all other qualities of the objects, and out of the many parts or degrees of straightness constructs the unity or one single idea of absolute straightness. It is therefore perfectly true that the senses do not perceive the absolutely or theoretically straight, they only perceive the special or separate parts of it; it is the understanding alone that perceives the *general* nature of straightness, but, of course, it could not do this without the material supplied by the senses. So, complete and absolute straightness is not something that exists first and from which all the less perfect parts are derived; on the contrary, it *consists of all the parts* of straightness, separated from other qualities and taken mentally as one whole; apart from these it has no existence. To say that a thing is straight is like saying a thing is right, neither statement has any meaning *unless we connect it with some purpose,* for example, we might say that a certain piece of wood is straight for the purpose of making a window-frame but not for testing a lathe bed.

The Exact Mathematical Unit. No two potatoes, men, scientific instruments or finely-wrought billiard balls are exactly alike, so where do we get the idea of exact equality between one and one, or between one hundred and one hundred, if all ideas are based on sense perceptions? If we break the idea of an abstract unit into its parts we find that the senses perceive varying degrees of what appears to be quantitative similarly in various objects. The understanding mentally separates these particular perceptions from those of weight, colour, etc., and by selecting the general element of equality from the varying degrees of approximate equality, constructs the idea of absolutely similar units of quantity. An absolutely exact unit is, therefore, not perceived by the senses (they perceive only the parts of the idea) but is produced by the understanding working with sense-perceived material, from which it mentally separates the general element of quantitative equality from all other parts of the universe. This absolute unit, then serves as the base for abstract calculations of all kinds, and is the abstract foundation of mathematical consistency or truth, though one should not forget that the whole range of mathematical reasoning *has no meaning unless applied to something practical,* when it is very quickly discovered that allowances have to be made; therefore, no such independent mathematical truth exists, as has been affirmed, except as a mental generalisation based on sense-perceived material. Those who speak of the eternal principles of the circle, the triangle, etc., and who think these principles *exist in things* independently of men's thoughts, are evidently unaware that every "single" thing *is a product of many things,* including thought; therefore, all principles are abstract generalisations of sense perceptions. It is no doubt a principle (to the mind that can understand it) that every circle contains three hundred and sixty degrees, but if the geometricians of the future take to milesimal measurements and decide to divide the circle into one thousand degrees, the three-sixty principle would vanish; of course, things would still be things if that is what is meant, but we already know the universe had no beginning and will have no end, and, therefore, "there will always and everywhere be matter"; what needs to be insisted upon is that things considered apart from thought *contain no principles,* for a principle must of necessity be a product of thought plus the things thought about. If geometricians have referred to such principles as "properties" of things and then gone on to imagine the existence of those "properties" independent of thought, it is time they studied logic.

Space and Time. The idea of space is an abstract generalisation constructed from sense perceptions of objects that are extended, such as houses, tables, etc., and that are said to occupy "space"; there is, of course, no separate entity which constitutes space. The idea of time is constructed in the same way from sense-perceived successions, such as one day following another, but there is no "thing" called "time" after the manner of Bergson. Space consists of its many parts. Time consists of its many moments. In each case the abstract unity is constructed from sense perceptions of concrete realities.

Force and Matter. Preliminary. Let us once again insist that the idea of distinguishing between different parts implies that such parts are *parts of one whole,* and, therefore, the universe as a whole is the logical starting point in any work of distinguishing. If we bear this in mind we guard against considering any part that we have separated and considered as a unit, as being a whole in itself apart from the rest of the universe, when in reality it is only our mental arrangement. Idealists have instinctively generalised force or energy and then treated it as though it was an altogether distinct and separate kind of thing; they have spiritualised it in the name of God or intangible Nature, whereafter it is God who makes railway engines move. The materialists of the narrow physical science school have gone the other way. They have mentally separated the ponderable matter from the force which is part of it, and then considered this distinction as absolute, with ponderable matter as the dominant partner in all their associations; whereafter it is ponderable matter that causes all things. Both have instinctively performed the mental separation, but have not been fully aware of what they have done, and all this because neither understands the science of understanding. Let us now analyse a few of the ideas occurring under the head of force.

Gravity. Breaking the idea of gravity into its parts, we see that the senses perceive parts of ponderable matter that appear to attract each other; they do not perceive the *general* force of gravity, it is the understanding that does this by mentally separating these particular phenomena of seeming attraction from all other qualities of ponderable matter, and then by adding them together, that is, generalising them, it constructs the single idea of gravity and gives it a name. Gravity *as a whole* is, therefore, perceived by the understanding and not by the senses, though the understanding could not do this if the senses did not perceive the separate parts of it. In objective reality outside the mind, gravity consists of the sum total of all its manifestations unseparated from the whole of the nature, *so it constitutes one of the parts of matter.*

Heat. The idea of heat when analysed shows heat to be nothing that exists by itself. It is seen as a whole only by the understanding which takes the separate sense perceptions of heat, such as those of the sun, a gas jet, a fire, an electric radiator or the result of any chemical action, mentally separates these parts from all other qualities of the sun, etc., and generalises them into one idea to which it gives the name of heat, thus mentally distinguishing between heat in *general* and all the special or particular parts of it. Of course, there is no such thing as heat apart from things that are heated, therefore, heat in general is an abstraction, while in objective reality it consists of all its parts *undetached from nature;* accordingly, *heat is one of the parts of matter.* " Hot " and " cold " are, of course, relative terms, so they must be *connected with some purpose,* that is, we must say what we are talking about before they can have any meaning; for example, water at 105° Fahr. may be hot for taking a bath but cold for cooking potatoes.

Light and Darkness. What is light? The sense of sight acquaints us with many manifestations of light. The understanding takes all these parts, and for the special purpose of discussing light, mentally separates them from all else and combines them into one general unit or idea of light. The senses acquaint us only with the separate parts, it is the understanding using these parts as its material that constructs the general nature of light, that is, light taken as a whole. There is, of course, no such thing as light existing by itself and which somehow or other pervades the rest of nature. In reality, outside the mind, light exists objectively only in the sum total of all its manifestations (all the beautiful colours we see), *it consists of these manifestations*, it is one of the parts of matter and is, therefore, not a something unknowable that remains at the back of the manifestations. Once we know how understanding performs its understanding it is clear that the general conception of light is simply the abstract or mental form of what exists in the concrete outside the mind in the totality of its separate manifestations undetached from matter.

But now, what is darkness? Darkness is the negation of light, and how can the senses perceive a negative? If all ideas are based on sense perception and the senses cannot perceive darkness where do we get the idea of it? If we remember that every unit, no matter how small, may be divided into still smaller parts, we shall see that light may be divided into different degrees of light, some of which are not so light as others. Those parts that present the greatest degrees of light are the parts from which the understanding constructs the *general* idea of light; the other parts which are not so light are the specials for the time being. But, just in the same way, the understanding may, if it wishes, take these specials and with them construct the idea of darkness, which, of course, constitutes their *general* nature, and in this case the greater degrees of light would constitute the special parts; in other words, what is special in one set of relationships may be general in others, or, the other way about. Wherefore, we see that darkness does not mean no light at all, nor does light imply no darkness at all. Light is the *general* nature of a relative lack of darkness, while darkness is the *general* nature of a relative lack of light; relative, that is, *to certain purposes,* for example, a certain degree of light might be quite light for reading large print but dark for taking photographs.

Sound and Silence. Analysing the idea of sound, we see the sounds of bells, drums, hammering, etc., to be separate manifestations of sound perceived by our sense of hearing. The understanding takes these separate perceptions or parts, mentally separates the sounds from all other qualities of the objects, and combines them into one idea, that of sound in general. Again, this *general* nature is not perceived by the senses but by the understanding working with the material supplied by the senses. With regard to silence, this idea does not arise from an *absolute* absence of sound, which obviously could not possibly be sense perceived; but as the *general character* of those degrees of sound that are relatively less noisy.

Motion and Stillness. What is motion? Let us analyse the idea in just the same way. We see men, machines, ships, clouds, in short, all kinds of bodies moving, we feel them moving, we come to know that *all* things are in motion. The understanding takes all these separate sense perceptions as one lot, separates this lot mentally from all other qualities possessed by the bodies, and then abstracts the general nature from all the separate motions, that is, it generalises their common features into the one idea of motion. It is, therefore, the understanding that perceives the general nature of motion, the senses perceive only the separate parts of it. Outside the mind, motion exists objectively in the sum total of the movements of all bodies, and is a part of matter; of course, there is no separate entity constituting motion, and which, so to speak, enters bodies or leaves them to go somewhere else.

Now, how about stillness? Think of a man sitting still in a railway train going at forty miles an hour on an earthly sphere that turns a complete revolution about its axis every twenty-four hours, meanwhile it is whirling around its orbit at about thirty miles a second, while some say the whole solar system is rushing headlong through space. From this it will be evident that stillness can only be conceived in a relative sense; for example, a man may sit still in a train in relation to other people or to the compartment in which he happens to be; or if two trains are running on adjacent lines in the same direction at the same speed, except for lateral vibration, one will be still in relation to the other, and so on; therefore, the idea of stillness is a generalisation from sense-perceived parts or instances of *relative* stillness. We can hear old-fashioned logic saying, "a thing in motion is in motion, it is not still, nor is it partly still," but our logic can explain how a thing can be still and yet in motion at one and the same time, just as a man may be living and dying at the same time.

Something and Nothing. That the idea of something is a generalisation from sense perceptions of things, surely needs no explanation; but how do we come by the idea of nothing? If we remember that the word "nothing" does not mean nothing at all but refers to those parts of existence that are relatively unimportant, as, for instance, when we speak of a bit of dust as being nothing, or a scratch on the hand as nothing, we shall see that the idea of nothing is simply a generalisation drawn from those parts of nature that are unimportant for the time being. This, despite the horror on the face of "Old Logic," teaches us that "nothing itself is something," for, considered as only an abstract generalisation, it is at least a thought, and thought is real.

Power. If the idea of power be analysed and resolved into its factors we shall see these to consist of sun power, horse power, wind power, man power, steam power, and so on. But, as in previous cases, the senses never perceive power in its totality. It is the understanding, using these sense perceptions as material, that mentally separates those many parts of power from all other qualities of the sun, horses, etc., and combines them into the one idea of *power in general.* Outside the mind, the total power consists of all the special parts of power, which are unseparated from objects *and accordingly form part of them;* there is no other power, so the idea of an Almighty power existing independently of nature, and which supplies power to nature, becomes a futility once we see that " universal power " is a mental concept built up from sense-perceived parts and that the parts are prior to the concept. Were there any other power *different from what we know as power,* it would require a different name to describe it, consequently it would not be power.

Force and Matter. Concluded. If heat, light, sound, feeling, seeing (sense stimuli), gravity, etc., are so many different manifestations of force, what is force itself? The physicists say we do not know, we only know its effects; they also say we do not know the ultimate nature of matter, though in recent years, by the electron theory already mentioned, they have resolved the atom into several thousands of electrons, supposed to be the product of electrical forces which neutralise each other and so produce points of electrical inertia expressing themselves as matter in the form of electrons. So matter is materialised energy, and energy is energised matter, the immaterial forces become material substances and *vice versa;* but, withal, we do not know the ultimate nature of the energy which *lies at the back* of its manifestations.

Now let us apply our logic. Every idea is composed of parts supplied by sense perception; the idea of force or energy is no exception. The special parts of the idea, or rather a few of them, we have already worked through, they consist of heat, light, power, etc. All these separate generalisations, based ultimately on sense perceptions, are taken by the understanding and treated by it as parts of a still wider generalisation which takes the form of force in total. But this total, or general force, does not exist apart from matter, it is not a separate entity that enters matter at one time and leaves it at another. It is only the mind's way of making distinctions that gives rise to that idea, for if we remember that matter consists of all its attributes taken together and that all these forces *are just such attributes* (matter without force is like matter without shape), it becomes plain that force in total is the same as matter in total, consequently there is nothing at all lying at the back of the manifestations of force, because it consists of those manifestations themselves. If we are dealing with the subject of force, we speak of material forces wherein matter is the predicate and force the subject; but if dealing with the subject of matter we speak of forceful matter, wherein force becomes the predicate and matter the subject; from which it should be clear that force is the same thing we call material nature, or the universe, the existence of which nobody doubts, because all know it to be a fact. What we seek to understand is not existence independent of the parts of existence which, of course, is nonsense, but the relations between those parts.

Scientists have long since done away with the supreme mind of God, but they are just as much at sea as theologians when dealing with the ultimate nature of force, including the human mind, particularly as it appears in the realms of morality, reason, spirit, the true, the good, the beautiful, etc. Not knowing logic, they operate in their own special sciences practically, that is, correctly as far as practice goes, but not with a full and consciously-applied theory of method; outside their own speciality, they do not work right even in practice. Even the ordinary working class reader (for whom this book has been written) may say regarding such examples of reasoning as water being hot for some purposes but cold for others, or it being light for reading but dark for photography, that this book tells him nothing, because he has already reasoned that way. Probably he is quite correct, for most people argue or reason well enough on small everyday matters, but, since they do not understand the *theory of thinking,* they do not see that *exactly the same method* should be employed in treating *all* questions, for just as what is hot for some things may be cold for others, so may some things be *right* for some people and *wrong* for others, and if the working class did its own thinking and employed for that purpose *a scientific method of approaching every question*, they would soon cease to be hoodwinked by the master class through accepting the point of view given them (often by leading scientists) in the daily press, the cinema, the church, the lecture-room, the political clubs and the trade union branch meeting, not to speak of wireless broadcasting; but, of rights and wrongs we shall see more in the next chapter.

CHAPTER XI

Logic applied to Mental and Moral Problems

Every truth must be the truth *concerning something,* otherwise it has no meaning and is no truth at all. In searching for the truth of anything we have, therefore, to first make clear what it is we are talking about, what the thing is, the purpose in view, etc., and then, with everything considered, to abstract the general nature or general agreement between the factors; if in this process we mentally combine too few factors our generalisation falls short of what is combinable outside the mind, or, to be more correct, in objective reality (thought itself may be objective), and we get error; if we take too many factors our generalisation overshoots the mark of objective reality, and again we get error. Assuming the reader agrees with the principles taught in the last two chapters and is prepared to apply the same method to all questions, we now proceed to consider a few mental and moral problems that are not usually treated scientifically, for it is in the field of the moral nature of man's reason where the greatest contention rages and where little or no science is applied. Take, first, the question of the reasonable.

The Reasonable. How do men know what is reasonable when they argue that five per cent. profit is reasonable, or that a certain standard of life is reasonable, or that the demands of capitalists are reasonable, or that workers demand unreasonably high wages, or that the present chaotic state of the world can never be set straight till men act towards each other with " a bit of reason "; what is the basis of their argument?

Since the understanding cannot operate without the senses, and the senses cannot function unless in contact with reality, it is clear that men, if they reason at all, *must reason about things,* and naturally they look upon things from the standpoint of whether or not they serve some need; *man's needs, therefore, lie at the bottom of man's reason.* Things that serve some need are sense perceived, and from such perceptions the understanding generalises the idea of the " reasonable "; while from sense perceptions of things that serve in a contrary direction the understanding generalises the idea of the " unreasonable." For example, on warm summer days men do not need to wear double-breasted overcoats; it would, therefore, be just as unreasonable to wear them at such times as it would be to neglect them in exceptionally cold weather. But it might be reasonable for an invalid to wear such a coat in summer, though his would be a special case; in like manner some individual might not need one even in cold weather, in which case it would be reasonable for him to go without, for again this would be a special case. Viewed in this way, that which is reasonable depends upon the needs of certain persons *with all the conditions taken into account;* vary the needs of the people, the times or the general conditions, and what was formerly reasonable will become unreasonable; accordingly, since the needs of different people are widely different, there can be no one thing or policy that is reasonable for all people at all times under all conditions.

To say it would be reasonable for all men to wear great coats on warm days because it was reasonable for the invalid to do so would be an error, because it would be making the special case into the general, it would be taking fewer factors than would be required to agree with reality. Truth being that statement that expresses the generality concerning any quantity of sense perceptions, it follows that it would be truly reasonable for the invalid to wear the coat because we are dealing only with his needs; the truth in this case would be a generalisation drawn from a small number of sense perceptions. Should we take a greater number of sense perceptions by considering the needs of people in general, it would be unreasonable to say they should all wear such coats at such times, because the invalid's case, although a general if taken by itself, becomes a special when taken in relation to a wider general.

Take another instance; the needs of people in general may be collectively expressed as the need to improve their position in life. Under the wages system, wage-workers need more wages to carry out this improvement, and this need leads them possibly to strike. But employers need more profits, which lead them to reduce wages and possibly to lock the workers out. Each section generalises its own needs, and what is reasonable for one is unreasonable for the other. So it is plain that the reasonable is reasonable only in relation to certain persons at certain times and under definite conditions; it is impossible for there to be anything that is universally reasonable under all conditions and for all persons. Moreover, since the needs of a small number of people within a given group constitute the special or unimportant needs as compared with the general needs of the group, it would be unreasonable for the smaller section to represent its special needs as being the general. On the other hand, if the larger section were too lavish in their generalising and included factors that were not applicable to their given problem, then their generalisation would not correspond with objective reality, *it would be too general for the given circumstances;* for example, if the majority of members of a trade union passed a resolution to the effect that reductions in wages were in the interest of both masters and men, or, if they preach that in general the interests of masters and men are alike, since the separate needs of masters on the one hand and workers on the other cannot be combined *in general practice,* such resolution or teaching is unreasonable, because more factors have been generalised inside the mind than can possibly be so in reality. To strive to reconcile capitalists and workers is unreasonable, because it is not in accord with objective reality (the capitalists deny this, but that is bluff), though it may be reasonable to attempt reconciliation *after* the contradiction of private ownership in means of production has been solved by social ownership, and the capitalist has become a mere man, that is, when the conditions have changed, but that, it must be borne in mind, is a different problem.

Take now an example of a different kind. Rationalists tell us it is unreasonable to believe in God, a future life, miracles, and so on. These people evidently do not understand logic; they imagine they get reason without sense perceptions, or, if they do not go quite so far as that, they at least elevate their own particular reason into *reason in general*. However, the people who worship God feel the need for prayer just as children feel the need for fairy stories, and in both cases it is a product of their reason that they should satisfy their need. Even a man who understands logic might quite reasonably read a book of fanciful poems, or go to a fanciful opera, or to a church service *if he likes those things and gets some degree of satisfaction from them*, but it would not be reasonable to attempt to solve political and economic questions with the information usually got from such sources, because, although it does not matter to the rest of men how he reasons privately or semi-privately among a small group, those reasons are small, unimportant, particular or special generalisations when considered in relation to politics and economics, for that which is reasonable in the latter spheres depends upon the needs of large groups, so, the political and economic needs being the *more widely general,* it becomes unreasonable to obtrude special religious notions; wherefore, we see once more that what is reasonable under some conditions, because general, becomes unreasonable under other conditions through having become the special in relation to a wider general. Since there may be readers who object to the idea of God's Holy religion being brought to the level of mere poetry or fairy lore, and who are still of the opinion that " sweet reasonableness " comes from on High and constitutes obedience to God's commands, it may be advisable to work through a few of the ideas contained in the greater idea of God.

Life. What is life? According to Genesis, God formed man out of clay. After finishing the model, "God saw that . . . it was very good," so He breathed "life" into it, whereupon the model became Adam. When Adam's body died, the breath of life departed and winged its way back to God; in fact, it belonged to God, or, rather, was part of Him all along.

This crude form of the idea has long since been discredited, nevertheless *its essential character remains* in many different forms, for modern philosophers are asking the questions, "What is life"? and "Why do we ascribe life to the living"? They seem to imagine that life is an entity of some kind that comes from somewhere, enters the body during the pre-natal period, only to leave it at death to go on living in some region after the body dies. Of course, there are variations on this theme, for some think of a soul that is not the life itself but which *possesses* life, though in actual conception there is little difference inasmuch as most people speak indiscriminately of the "immortal soul" and "immortal life."

The idea of life, like all ideas, is built up of parts consisting of sense perceptions of the many separate instances of life, such as animals, trees, microbes, etc.; the brain separates the sense perceptions of life from the sense perceptions of all other qualities of the animals, etc., and generalises them into the one idea of life in total. Life is not a thing, but a function of matter, and the understanding gives this function a name to distinguish it from other functions of matter.

In reality, outside the mind, life consists of the sum total of the many different instances of life. There is no separate thing called "life" that may enter the body, or leave it and still go on living. Such an idea is a mere mental abstraction, a unity that exists in the mind only, there being no corresponding unity outside the mind.

Through not understanding how the brain works, people have performed the generalisation practically, but have not understood it theoretically; this has led them to treat the abstraction as an entity, so it is no longer wonderful to find that living things have " life," indeed it would be peculiar if we did not ascribe life to the living seeing that we get our general idea of it from sense perceptions of those same living things. Looked at like this it is no more wonderful that certain combinations of matter should exhibit the function called life than that other combinations should exhibit other functions; for example, that a lucifer match should burst into flame on being scratched by sand paper; each particular combination of matter exhibits its particular function, so we employ different names to describe the different functions.

Every part of matter changes the manner of its functioning with every change in its physical constitution; for example, a man's body is gradually dying at the same time that it is living, but we distinguish between living and dying *by separating the special from the general.* If a body is building up new parts more quickly than old parts decay (both processes are results of changes in its physical constitution), the building-up process is more *general* than the decaying process, so the decaying relates to a smaller quantity of material changes, it is consequently the special in this case, and we say truly that the body is living because that is its *general* character. After a body has reached maturity it begins to decay more rapidly than it builds up; it is then in the dying stage, because the decay is becoming more general than its opposite; when the decay has reached such a point that building up *in the form of that particular organism* ceases, then the dying process has become very general, and we truly state the body to be dead. We should never forget that decay itself *is but the building up of new forms of matter.* University logic would say life is not death, nor is it partly so, for life and death are opposite terms; but our logic shows them to be *one process,* the different parts of which are separated entirely by the mind working with sense perceptions. To ask " what is the ' life force ' apart from the remainder of living matter " is like asking " what is explosive force apart from matter that is exploding, or freezing force apart from ice "?

Robert Blatchford has quite recently again made the old remark, that when a man is struck dead with a cannon ball the chemical elements are still there but the body is no longer living, and asks, " What is it that has gone "? We answer, it is the particular arrangement of the parts that has gone, which arrangement was necessary to enable the chemicals to function in the way we describe as living, just as in case the cannon ball had struck a house and reduced it to ruins, the bricks and mortar would still be there but lack of the required arrangement would prevent them from functioning by way of giving shelter (in ridicule we might even ask what has become of the " shelter " apart from the bricks and mortar—shall we meet it again in the Great Beyond?). In the former case we no longer call the body a man, nor in the latter case do we call the bricks and mortar a house, because in each case *the general nature* has been changed, and so we require a different name to describe it. If the argument be advanced that we could rebuild the house but not the man, we should say this was merely a question of the extent of the damage in either case, coupled with the relative skill on the part of the doctors and of the builders. In case the damage is too extensive to be repaired, a new house might be built, or a new man be produced, by taking the action appropriate in either case.

Immortality. This idea has for its parts just the same as life, but with other parts added to them, such as the continuity of functioning running through living organisms taken as a whole throughout history, the desire of every conscious organism to live as long as it can, the desire for continued companionship, the idea of a stable condition of things which takes no notice of the continual change, the desire for rest and peace when one feels tired of work, the hurly-burly of life or the agony of prolonged sickness and suffering, and so on. When a man says " I wish I were dead " he means (usually) nothing of the kind, rather does he feel a desire to be free from his present trouble, and if the only possible way is by parting with his body, then he is willing to pay that price, but he has the idea of still going on living. We, therefore, see the idea of Immortality to be an abstract generalisation from sense perceptions of parts of the universal being that are not so generalised outside the mind; it is consequently an error.

Perfection. In life, people perceive by the aid of their senses that some machines work more accurately than others; that some persons are more refined than others, or more generally useful to society, nicer to get on with, easier to talk to, and so on; that some books as compared with others are easier to read and contain more beautiful language; also a thousand-and-one other excellences. Now, it will be quite evident that what is desirable or nice for one person will not be equally so for all. Each person takes his own circle of sense perceptions, singles out what is for him the *generally desirable,* and calls it the perfect, whereafter this becomes *his* standard of perfection, while his standard of imperfection consists of the *general character* of the undesirable. There are, of course, no such things as " perfection " in itself, " beauty " in itself, " good " in itself, and so on; otherwise we might ask " Why have last year's beautiful fashions become ugly "?

But these individual concepts are not the end of the question, for such separate generalisations come in conflict with one another through conversation or comparisons of various kinds, thereby leading to a more extended idea which becomes a generalisation drawn from a wider circle; it may be in style of dress, manner of address, style of writing, deportment, knowledge, etc. From all these separate and relatively small generalisations, there are brains that generalise the idea of a complete and absolute perfection contrasted with its opposite complete imperfection.

With our explanation we see these latter ideas to be mere mental abstractions, the unity exists in the mind only, there being no corresponding unity outside the mind. It is not the senses that perceive perfection but the understanding, though it could not do this without the material supplied by the senses. Outside the mind the only perfection that exists is contained in the many concrete instances of perfection which themselves consist of small mental generalisations of sense-perceived facts, having for their base that which is admirable because desirable. Therefore, *human wants lie at the bottom of the absolutely perfect*, it being nothing but the abstract mental reflection of the general desires of mankind.

Freedom and Will. What is freedom? By their senses men perceive that they may move from place to place, they may write letters, they may make wealth, they may be lazy, etc. Throughout all such-like they feel they are choosing one line of action in preference to another, and when they have done something they feel they could have done otherwise had they wished, and that accordingly they are free to choose; from all these sense perceptions the understanding generalises the idea of freedom. But what are sense perceptions? Do they not imply a relation between that which perceives and that which is perceived? Evidently these apparently free acts are expressions of the relations between the individual and the rest of nature and his acts *are a product of both.* This being so they cannot be called free any more than a cork can be called free when, on being released at the bottom of a tank of water, it rises to the surface. The movement of the cork is determined (not pre-determined) by both itself and the water, and so are men's acts determined in like manner.

Man's needs, again, lie at the bottom of this question; he requires the necessaries of life, and in order to live it is necessary that he exert himself to get them. This necessary exertion is already implied *in the fact* of existence for without such striving there would be no existence at all, the *idea* of existence is *but the abstract form of all that is.* Man's acts are, therefore, nothing but the carrying into effect of all the *necessary* relations between himself and the rest of nature, and are

THINKING

consequently determined at each given moment. This necessity appears in the form of a series of impulses to do certain things; those impulses that are strongest within a man at any given moment are executed, provided there are no combinations of outside forces sufficient to stop him; at these times he experiences the feeling of freedom and, of course, in the reverse case, lack of freedom. Since only those impulses that are strongest or quantitatively superior can prevail, it follows again that the expression of what is called the " human will " is only the expression of the general over the particular. *From separate sense perceptions of numerous carryings out* of such strong impulses, the understanding generalises the idea of the human " will," whereafter that generalisation is regarded as a mysterious entity, and is called the " will "; but we see there is no such entity in reality, either outside the mind or even inside, except the mental abstraction.

Since all things are *necessary* parts of existence, " freedom " is nothing but a name for the expression of the strongest forces, and is, of course, relative to those forces. For example, each rising political class makes its demands in the name of " freedom " or " liberty " as an appeal to an " eternal " principle; when it gets sufficient force to achieve power it is said to have acquired freedom, whereafter it styles its particular country a " free " country, while it itself becomes conservative in order to preserve its own particular brand of freedom. Since any particular freedom is conditioned by force, so-called unconditional freedom such as is implied in the Holy Will of God is an error, it is the elevation of numerous particular wills into the general, which is afterwards considered as detached from and independent of nature.

As thought is one of the material parts of man, and as a man at any given moment is simply a combination of material factors which *must act according to its constitution,* then to give a man a new thought obviously varies the combination, and so will he act in a different way (thinking is an act), just as will gunpowder, in the presence of a spark, act in different ways according to whether or not it is combined with water. Assuming a thousand impulses to act in a certain way, and a similar number of similar strength to act in some other definite way, equilibrium takes place regarding those particular ways of acting, though one additional impulse on either side may be enough to upset the balance. This principle may be seen at work in propaganda, education, advertising, scolding, hypnotism, etc., etc. In all these cases the acting principle is that of suggestion, either auto or non-auto, and it would seem that those modern psychologists, who are interested in what has been erroneously called "Couéism," are coming to realise this when they ask "is the imagination (thought) stronger than the will?"

If the foregoing is true, then it becomes quite scientific to tell oneself repeatedly what one intends or wishes to do, for as soon as the repeated stimulus has acquired sufficient accumulated subconscious strength, or developed a new neurone pattern, the individual *must* respond, of course within the limits to which thought is operative, for we must remember that thought is only *one* part of the universe. Faith *considered as faith* has nothing to do with the matter, but considered as thought it is operative like all thought.

The writer feels that the sooner psychologists drop the "will" overboard the better; there will then be a clear field in which to develop the practice of suggestion on scientific lines, the inapplicability of the idea of "will" is at present a stumbling block.

Knowledge. What is knowledge? The idea of knowledge is a generalisation drawn from sense perceptions of the different parts of knowledge possessed by everybody and everything that knows anything at all, that is clear. From our previous work it will also be clear that there is no knowledge without sense perception; for there is no other kind of knowledge besides that which we know as knowledge, if there were it would require a different name, and consequently would not be knowledge. Again, knowledge can only be known by *brains that are dependent on sense perceived material*, otherwise knowledge would be the knowledge of nothing; so there can be no knowledge of all the past and the future, that is, of eternity " from the beginning unto the end."

God. To analyse the idea of God we must follow the rules of our logic in just the same manner as before. We think of God as being the source of life, or as being life itself; as being without beginning or end, and therefore immortal; as being completely perfect; as being that which is all good; as being omnipotent or all powerful, omniscient or all knowing, and omnipresent or everywhere at once; as being eternally just, eternally loving, eternally merciful, eternally angry, eternally mild and, at least as far as Christians are concerned, as having the form of a human being inasmuch as " God made man in his own image." Now realising that all ideas must necessarily be based upon sense perceptions, we see that God is a mental generalisation of a great number of smaller generalisations, all of which we have seen to consist, in their parts, of the abstract form of man's material relations between himself and other natural objects. And since this mental combination does not exist *as a combination* outside the human head, notwithstanding that its parts exist and are separately sense perceived, it follows that we perceive God with our understanding merely as an abstraction. See Fig. 5. He is, in fact, abstract man carried to infinity; so we may truly say that " Man made God in his own image."

Morality and Right. Our logic is the one and only guide that can conduct us safely through the maze of the moral. In war time it is right to kill, to tell lies about the enemy, etc.; in peace time it is considered wrong. Polygamy is moral in Eastern countries, in Western countries it is immoral. But among the many notions of morality there is one general outstanding feature common to them all—they all serve some *general need* pertaining to a certain society or group within a society; and if we take any such group, consider

164   THINKING

its interests and find out what is its general need, we shall have found what is truly moral for that particular group.

Let us start with one man. If a man lives entirely by himself he makes his own morals, or to be more correct,

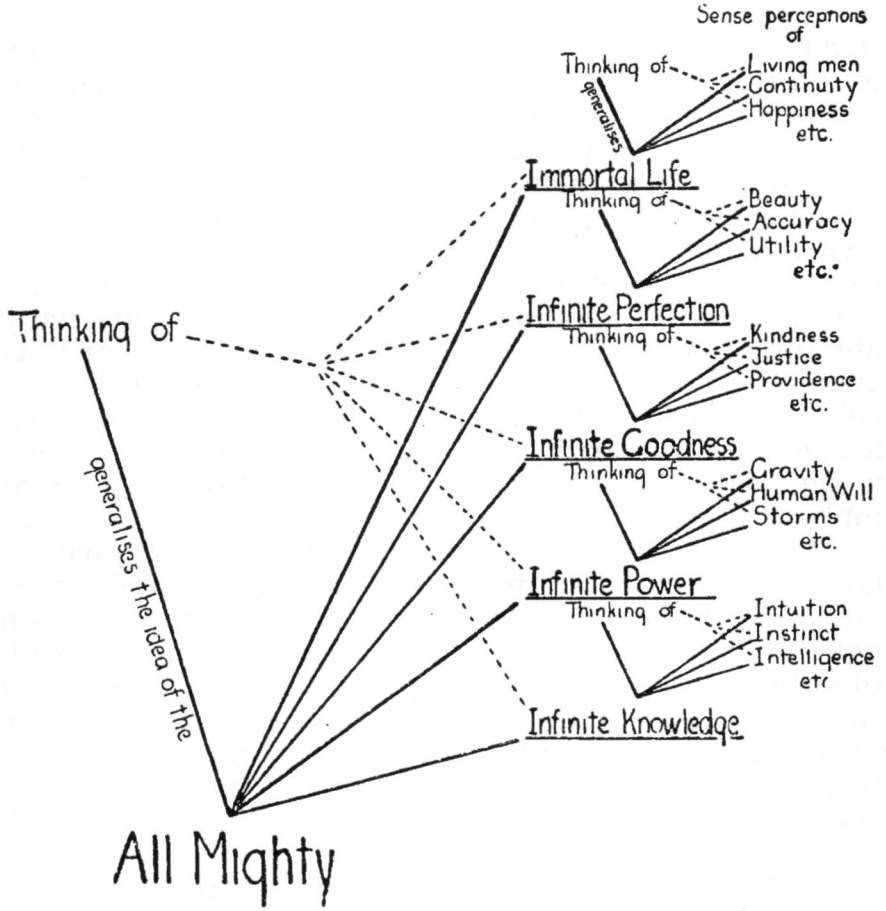

                            Sense perceptions of
              Thinking of — Living men
                         Continuity
                         Happiness
                           etc.
            Immortal Life
              Thinking of — Beauty
                         Accuracy
                         Utility
                           etc.
Thinking of —   Infinite Perfection
              Thinking of — Kindness
                         Justice
                         Providence
                           etc.
            Infinite Goodness
              Thinking of — Gravity
                         Human Will
                         Storms
                           etc.
            Infinite Power
              Thinking of — Intuition
                         Instinct
                         Intelligence
                           etc
            Infinite Knowledge

All Mighty

Fig. 5. Diagrammatic suggestion of the construction of the thought of God, from sense perceptions of objective reality.

the question of morality as generally, and therefore truly, understood does not arise, for the reason that he cannot have any relations with other people. But, if he lives with another man they each have to respect the other's needs, and if one is a pugilist while the other is a weakling, then, in any matter of dispute, the morality is finally dictated by the pugilist; though if the work or, maybe, the companionship of the weakling is necessary for the well being of the pugilist, the pugilist must take this into consideration for his own sake. While each man has likes and dislikes peculiar to himself, these are only special needs and do not count, it is therefore their common or general needs that determine their morality, and this at any moment of serious difference between them turns upon the will of the pugilist, because he is able to coerce his partner if necessary (" I'm the boss here, I'll tell you what's right "). Coercion, though, is not always pugilistic in character; it might be that the weakling is a weakling in the body, but very cunning and superior mentally (analogous to the capitalist class and the working class). Assuming this, it would be possible for him to demonstrate his mental might by " educating " the pugilist " in the way he should go," unless the pugilist should " educate himself " from his own standpoint. In either case, whichever particular morality obtained, it would only be the mental generalisation of sense perceptions which, of course, depend upon the material conditions governing their lives; should these change the morality changes. It is evident, then, there is no morality that is right for all people and for all time.

To take another example. We go to the theatre, where we are in company with a number of people who desire entertainment, and have therefore a common need. If among the audience there should be a drunken man, who persists in being a nuisance, the general body assert their morality in calling for his removal, and, if necessary, that morality is demonstrated by the man being forcibly ejected.

That which is moral is, accordingly, that which serves the general needs of certain groups of people at certain times and places; and the nature of morality is the upholding of the general interest over the particular.

As sense perceptions vary with variations in the material or economic conditions to which different nations at the same time or the same nation at different times are subject, so do different moralities exist as between different countries at the same time or within a given country at different times (the same remarks apply to different classes within a country). For example, the morality of the Dark Ages was that of the Catholic Church and Feudal Barons, and its might consisted theoretically of the threat of Hell, and practically of the sword and torture. When the Church and the nobles were in the strongest position they were the dictators, as an instance, usury was immoral; but when the economic mode of production changed and brought development of trade, there arose *new needs* based on the new material conditions. The old nobility fought to retain its supremacy, but as the rising capitalist class increased in numbers their growing *might* gradually asserted itself; this might was that of monetary power, which, with the need for foreign markets in which to dispose of the increased product of machine work, translated itself into extensions of military and naval power culminating in imperialism and "the honour of the Flag." All these changes were accompanied by different moralities; for example, with the banking system, usury became moral, at least to the extent of the usual rate of interest; the virtues included thrift and abstinence, solvency for those who paid and bravery for those who fought, and all this, be it remembered, in the name of the Holy will of God. Each powerful class claims that its morality is based upon "eternal" right, "eternal" justice, and so on; but our logic exposes the fact that there is no "eternal" or "absolute right," it shows us that morality is relative to persons, times and places, for every so-called "absolute right" is really *the might of a particular class* enforcing its particular desires regarding its particular *needs*. From this it will be easily seen how powerful can be the lever of education in the hands of a governing class, and also how necessary it is for the working class *to educate itself* from its own particular standpoint.

In so far as the development of capitalism is ever increasing the number of workers, and relatively thinning the ranks of the capitalists, so are the needs of the capitalist class becoming the particular, while the needs of the working class are becoming the general. Working class morality is slowly taking form, but before it can obtain general recognition it will have to be expressed in the economic might of the workers in expropriating the capitalists by socialising the means of production. This is why capitalists are so desperately anxious to " educate " the working class in the direction of conciliation and " impartiality."

Holiness. Since morality is determined by the superior power or might of the general over the particular, then *the general needs become the end in view,* and, provided the end as conceived in the abstract is a correct generalisation of the general needs, which correctness can only be attained by a study of all the factors concerned, so may we say that the end is justified. Of course, there is no such thing as an end considered by itself, for like every other single idea, the idea of an end is built up of sense perceptions, consequently all " ends " are constructed by the understanding in relation to the material conditions out of which they are generalised.

So also with the idea of the " means " to attain a given " end." If the end is justified, so are the means; but since the end in view cannot be attained without the necessary means, we see that the end when realised is only the sum of all its means taken together, consequently means do not exist in themselves, but are only means when taken in relation to some definite end, for should the end in view not be realised, then what were expected to be the means to that end never become means, therefore means are only relative.

If human welfare be taken as the end in view, then all actions toward that end become means, and the end being the *whole* welfare, is the Holy. But if we analyse the idea of the whole well-being of the human race, we find it to be composed of parts; for example, the production of food, clothing, entertainment, the acquisition of knowledge, etc. These parts are the means of attaining the end in view, and taken altogether constitute that end. Though if we take one of those parts or "means" and consider it by itself, we find it is an "end" which has its own special means; for example, taking the production of food as the end in view, its parts or means consist of the separate acts involved in agriculture, cattle raising, and so on. Therefore, the relatively small or particular means of agriculture, etc., taken together constitute the "end" of food production, and likewise the particular means employed in science, taken together, constitute the "end" in view, science. But food and science, which are "ends" in relation to their special means, themselves become the "means" of the greater "end" of human welfare. So, the whole welfare of the human race, or the Holy, is the only absolute end, *all other ends being relative.* Wherefore it follows that if any group of persons having a special end in view call it the Holy, they are wrong, and the means they employ are wrong. For example, the end that capitalists have in view is profit, and the means they employ are the private ownership of factories, tools, etc., and the purchase of labour power. These factors express themselves in capitalist politics, capitalist authority, the capitalist State, capitalist law, capitalist war, and capitalist education for workers, inculcating the doctrines of thrift, increased production, fighting for the Flag, etc., but, above all, hard work for relatively low wages. "It is the holy will of God that the poor must work." "It is a grievous wrong and a sin to attack the *sanctity* of private property." But evidently, since the end in view, namely, profit, can only serve *the need of a particular class,* then it cannot be *general* or whole, or Holy. Although capital was justified in its day because it made wealth to flow like water, and so tended as a step towards the ultimate *general* good, it is no longer justified, because it is holding back the general product from the general mass of the people who produce it. Therefore, if profit as an end in view is no longer justified, neither are its means, the private ownership of the property used in producing it, or, in a word, the wages system.

Here more than anywhere else we see the necessity of

teaching logic to the working class, and also the reason why university professors, who belong directly or indirectly to the capitalist class, *dare not teach it*. " It is a holy and a wholesome thought " not " to pray for the dead," but to teach the living, though almost starving, mass of workers to reject the spurious Holiness offered them by their masters, whether in press, pulpit or parliament.

CHAPTER XII

Various Examples of Applied Logic

One who adopts the Science of Understanding as outlined in the last three chapters will agree that no single thought is possible without a basis of sense perception, and, therefore, to trace our thoughts back far enough, invariably ends in establishing the relationship that always exists between the knowing brain and the object which is known. The method is very simple, but the acquisition of material upon which to use it means work, as it involves a study of all those things we wish to examine, for without the necessary material we are left guessing, and the difference between guessing and science is, of course, the difference between chancing our luck and certainty. The scientific method consists of splitting every question into its essential ideas, then splitting each idea into its sense perceived parts and comparing our mental work with what exists outside the mind, that is, comparing the abstract existence of things with their concrete existence. By this means we may see which generalisations are objectively possible and which are not, or, in other words, the difference between the general and the special, or, again, between truth and error. Having learned the method, we now proceed to apply it to those questions tabulated in the first chapter, not as yet answered; in doing this it is, of course, assumed that the reader is sufficiently familiar with economic and social science.

What is True Democracy? Here are two ideas, " truth " and " democracy." Truth is that which is general within a given circle, so much we already know. Democracy means the rule of the people, or that the whole of the people rule themselves. But, dividing this idea into its parts, we see it to be impossible as an objective generalisation, for how can the people be said to rule themselves while they are divided into two classes, workers and capitalists, whose *separate general needs* are opposed? It must of necessity be the rule of one class. The voting of the working class, although it constitutes a small mental training for the future, nevertheless, at present is no more than a hoodwinking device, and must remain so till the might is abolished that arises from the private ownership of the means of production (factories, railways, etc.), upon which is based *capitalist morality*. This morality preaches the sanctity and inviolability of such private property. The capitalist class accordingly elevates a *partial* good, *the realisation of its own general needs* into *the general good of all people,* and hypocritically preaches the idea of democracy as one of the means towards its own end.

There is, therefore, no such thing as true democracy, nor can there be under class rule. The idea exists as a generalised abstraction in people's minds; it is based upon facts that are sense perceived, but since these facts are not capable of being generalised outside the mind so long as capitalism lasts, the generalisation is for the present untrue because *it is too general for the existing conditions.*

Would the Practice of Humanitarian Principles be good for Society? This question presupposes (1) that general humanitarian principles exist, (2) that we can at the present time speak intelligently of the good of society, and (3) that the practice of such assumed principles is possible.

(1) " Humanitarian principles " are mental abstractions based upon sense perceived facts that relate to human beings. Since the material conditions of various groups are very different from each other, so are their sense perceptions, and likewise consequently their

mental generalisations, as witness those of Englishmen, Turks, Negroes, and so on; from the various partial generalisations the understanding draws a wider generalisation, that of the abstract " absolutely humanitarian," which has no corresponding existence outside the mind; the parts of it exist outside the mind, but not the combination, it is therefore too general.

(2) The " good of society " is another abstraction to which the same remarks apply.

(3) Since no abstract idea can be put into practice unless it corresponds with reality outside the mind, it follows that even within these limits the practice of humanitarian principles turns, not upon their being humanitarian, *but upon the material conditions obtaining at any given time;* and if the advocates of such humanitarianism wish to show the superiority of their principles they must be prepared to enforce them and to demonstrate their morality *by might.*

Of course, just as a certain group think their special ideas are correct because they are in accord with the " eternal principles of truth and humanity," so do groups whose interests lie in the opposite direction appeal to the same principles to justify their opposition, which shows that the principles advocated by each group, when reduced to the concrete, are *special* to each group. *Each calls them the general* and tries to bluff the other by speaking of them as Holy, that is, pertaining to the whole, when in reality they are *partial,* and have to rest upon force for their application. To say " if one man holds such principles, so could all men if only they would " ignores the fact that ideas are determined by material conditions, which include the faculty of thinking, so that we cannot ourselves choose what we think. Therefore, humanitarian principles, considered in the light of what is ordinarily meant when the term is used, are simply beautiful soap bubbles requiring nothing beyond our logic to demonstrate their emptiness.

With regard to the application of Christian principles in solving social problems, the same remarks apply. Since Christian principles emanate from a sect, "advanced" thinkers and orators throw them overboard as being too narrow, they claim that their ideas are not the silly sectarian ones, but are broad-based on the principles of humanity, and so do they succeed in showing the same kind of silliness in the lump.

All ideals have a material base, whether they be true or false, but they are useful only when they correspond with those material conditions that may make their realisation possible. Outside this, they may be pleasant dreams and quite harmless, provided they are not taken seriously; but when they are, much waste of time ensues, and they become a sub-conscious but impracticable nuisance. Our logic, it must be remembered, does not exclude the delights of poetic or even political imagination, such as communistic thoughts of the future or I.L.P. policies with regard to the present, but simply shows such imagination in its true light, thereby keeping it from clogging the wheels of practical affairs. True enough, without imagination much would be missed, but, then, many things are better missed, so we should learn to discriminate.

Is Education good for the Working Class? Education is a means to an end, if the end is justified, so are the means; here we have to split up the ideas of "education" *considered as a means,* and "the good of the working class" *considered as an end;* and an end to be good must serve some need.

We know that workers need to live, as do non-workers; and that progress consists in maintaining or improving a given standard of comfort, intellectual or otherwise, with an ever decreasing expenditure of energy; consequently all education that tends towards this end is good for the working class. But we also know that in capitalist countries the people are divided into the capitalist class and the working class. Capitalists, living without producing wealth, have needs opposed to those of the workers, and since they control all general education they necessarily permeate that education with ideas that serve their class needs, because those ideas necessarily appear to them as good; therefore, while the general nature of education is good for workers, that special permeation is bad.

To counteract this capitalist speciality, it is necessary for workers to develop a type of education consistent with their own special needs, at the same time that they partake of education in its more general character. Our logic shows that both these special types of education are small generalisations which, being opposed in practice, cannot be unified, though the abstract unity may obtain inside the mind as an error; nor at the present time can either speciality taken separately be an integral part of the general. Each class strives to demonstrate the truth of its special generalisation, the one conservative the other revolutionary. Now, owing to the inexorable working of economic laws, whereby the working class are becoming more numerous and more dependent, the workers' educational speciality s gradually becoming more and more general; it leads to an abstract ideal of the social ownership of factories, tools, materials, and the mechanism of distribution and exchange. Whenever this ideal is realised in the concrete, the special working-class character of education (excluding the purely propagandist sides) will become part of *general* education, and thereby its truth will be demonstrated. The education given to workers by capitalists is conservative as considered from their special standpoint, while pretending to be impartial, because it tends to confuse the issue between the two classes, but they cannot help it being progressive considered from general standpoints; this essential contradiction will be solved by the conservative side being exposed as a result of the progressive element enabling workers to read for themselves.

We may conclude, then, that the *general* education which tends towards greater production with less expenditure of energy, is good for workers when separated from the *special* capitalist ideas running through it, because it makes for *general* progress; but for the same reason special, partial or Independent Working-Class Education is good for workers because, first, it leads to a more correct generalisation of their own *special needs,* and, second, shows that as economic development proceeds, it must eventually become part of a wider general. Consequently the special capitalist class character of general education is wrong for workers, *because it persists in elevating the former's special interests or special good into the general good* which it can never become.

If Socialism is bound to come of what use are Classes in Social Science? This question pre-supposes for the sake of argument that the human will is determined or not free, or to put it another way, that the idea of "the will" is nothing but a mental generalisation from sense perceived impulses just as we have previously described, and then by implication *goes on to suppose that we have free wills* and *could* sit down and do nothing by using those wills. The fallacy exists *in the question itself.*

If *all* our acts are determined, so are the acts of class teaching determined, and those who are so constituted, other conditions permitting, cannot avoid conducting classes. Of course, we could, and as a matter of fact would, sit down and do nothing if we wished, but the outstanding feature is that we cannot wish that way, for the material conditions governing our lives compel us to act *in some way,* and the particular way is determined by our mental generalisations of sense perceived facts, for we cannot get knowledge in any other way. Time was when people thought that some things tended to rise and some to fall, but the theory of gravitation offers a much better explanation by taking as its starting point the idea that *all* things are attracted towards each other, whereby they are saved from wasting time trying to find out which things tend to fall and which to rise, without things being any different *in fact,* for gravity had operated all the time on all things, prior to the discovery of its general law. And just in the same way the knowledge that the human will is nothing but an abstract idea built up from sense perceptions of those impulses that are strongest, saves us from foolishly wasting time trying to discover how far our acts are determined and how far they are free, without in the least altering the way in which man, including the rest of nature, develops, for this has been operative at all times just like the principle of gravity. Those who argue that the human will is free within limits, a freedom analogous to that of a bird within the limits of its cage, might as well argue, as in our previous illustration, that a cork in water is free from the influence of gravity when it rises to the surface of the water which limits its rising capacity.

If it be granted that the general statement of determinism (not pre-determinism or fatalism) is true, how do we account for those individuals who have developed inertia consequent upon holding the idea that socialism is inevitable? It is simply that the thought, sense perceived, has been one of the determining influences which, taken altogether, establish a balance of impulses and consequent inaction *in that particular line* (a balance in all lines at the same time is impossible, for we *must* act in some way); the practical corrective (from the writer's standpoint) for this state of mind is economic pressure direct or indirect on that particular individual to which he will or rather *must* respond one way or another, although it might, and sometimes does, result in suicide; the theoretical corrective is, of course, a study of logic. (The special and the general as relating to this question have already been dealt with under Freedom and Will, page 161.)

Would it be right for Socialists to confiscate the Property of Capitalists, or, is it right to Steal? This question, like very many others, betrays an unconscious mixing up of ideas in that it pre-supposes the socialisation of the means of production, and stealing, to be one and the same thing; as they are quite different we must answer the two questions separately.

(1) Is it right to steal?

The idea of stealing can arise only on the basis of privately-owned property, and its parts consist of numerous sense perceptions of acts wherein certain persons appropriate to their own uses, property which by common consent belongs to other people. All morality is based upon the needs of mankind, and the serving of the *general* needs of any special part of mankind is ensured *by might;* there can be no morality that transcends this, for " eternal " rights, even though strongly advocated, are of no avail, therefore, since there is nothing that is right " in itself," where stealing serves some general need and is *generally* considered right, it is right, and where *generally* considered wrong, it is wrong.

Among early communal tribes it was quite common to regard stealing from some other tribe as the proper thing to do, while within the tribe, where things were held in common, the idea could not apply; but as private property developed inside the tribe, then, for the *general* good of the tribe, stealing was considered immoral inside while it still remained moral to steal from outside. As tribes joined together to form nations the immorality of stealing became extended with the *greater generalisation of the common need*, though it was still moral to steal from other nations when needs decreed so, as in the stealing of oil, coal, rubber, iron, etc., always, of course, under some transcendental guise as " for the greater honour and glory of God," or " in the interests of civilisation and progress." But with the wages system the human race has been divided into wage-workers and capitalists, which alters the question of stealing the means of production into that of socialising them.

(2) Would it be right to socialise the means of production?

This question, like the previous one, can arise only on the basis of privately-owned property, but not until that property has gone through a long course of historical development and has arrived at the point where it is against the *general* need, inasmuch as the workers are the most numerous but, speaking relatively, fare very badly; and this under conditions that are technically capable of providing equitably for all.

The idea of socialisation is a mental generalistion arising from many sense perceptions of the fact that ownership of the product depends upon ownership of the means of producing it; and since the workers constitute the *general* mass of the people they see that the *general needs* of the human race concerning wealth, production, and distribution can be served only by the *social* ownership of factories, tools, railways, etc. The conservative owning class speak of socialisation as stealing, they make their *special* needs (profit) into the *general* and say " stealing is wrong in the sight of God and man " (except when they go to war for new markets and raw materials). They do not rely, however, merely on the preaching of this abstract principle, but rather on the physical force of military and police. On the other hand, sentimental socialists say that the means of life are the " free gifts of God " and ought to belong to all men. What these people do not see is that their abstract contention can only be realised *by might,* the might of an economically-organised working class. So, because it is in the interests of the *general* welfare, it becomes right to think of socialising the means of production, and since the end is justified so are the means to that end. The idea of paying for them is absurd, for, according to the most liberal estimates, the working class receive only a quarter of the product, and this must be consumed in order to keep them alive.

For those who see no difference between socialising and stealing, we must point out that stealing implies the complete dispossession of the former owner, while socialisation implies joint ownership. It is, therefore, right to socialise the means of life in general, but wrong to steal property not included in those means, because the former serves *a general need,* the latter only a *special one.*

Why is Evil Desirable? Nothing is evil in itself or good in itself. All acts are performed with the intention of serving man's needs, no matter how depraved those needs may be as viewed from other people's standpoints. Those acts which serve general needs are sense perceived, whereupon we mentally separate those parts of the acts which give general satisfaction, from all other parts, and add them together into the one idea of goodness. On the other hand, all acts which, though they may serve *individual* or special needs, yet are opposed to the *general* good, are similarly sense perceived and their common features generalised by the understanding into the idea of evil. There may, of course, be any number of generals, each of which becomes a special in relation to a greater general; for example, one kind of food may be good for one member of a family but bad for the family in general; or what one whole family may consider good for itself may be generally bad for some organisation to which it belongs; similarly, what may be good for that particular organisation may be bad for the class to which it belongs, and finally, what may be good for one class may be bad from the general standpoint of the whole of the people. Evil is that which is particular or special from the standpoint of any given general view, while good is that general itself. Therefore, evil is desirable because it is good within a relatively small circle, and within this circle it is good because it serves some need.

Is Machine Production Beneficial for Society? We had better know what we are talking about before we start, for we cannot get a solution unless we know the limits of the question; therefore we must mark off the circle of phenomena we wish to investigate. If by "machine production" we mean the machine production *of commodities* (the words could mean many other things; for example, astronomical observations with an equatorial telescope, current coins turned out from the Mint, gramophone tunes, etc.), the question becomes clear, and all we need do is to split it into its essential ideas, then take each one separately and split it into its parts to see how the generalisations arise. It is only after this process has been gone through that we can get an accurate solution, for only then can we see whether or not the generalisations correspond with reality; though we may, and occasionally do, get right by accident so far as our awareness is concerned. After limiting the question to the machine production of commodities, the essential ideas are "beneficial" and "society." From the standpoint of commodity production and the distribution of the product, the idea of "society" is an abstract generalisation that embraces too much, seeing that society is divided into workers and capitalists whose economic interests are opposed; the idea, accordingly, does not correspond with reality, nor can it so long as the conflicting interests are facts; therefore, in this connection the word "society" is an error. With regard to the idea of "benefit," that which is beneficial must be sense perceived as *serving some need*, and if we analyse these needs we shall find the limitations within which the term can be accurately employed.

Assume an individual who owns a machine that enables him by its output to withdraw from the socially-produced surplus value a greater amount of that value in money form than he contributes in commodity form, obviously that would be *specially* good for him but *generally* bad for the others. The same applies to group ownership within the capitalist class, for the success of one group would be *special* as compared with the *general needs* of the whole class. But now, taking the whole capitalist class as a general by itself, since profit (surplus value) is socially produced, that is, by the combined total capital, then in proportion as the application of machinery extends their field of exploitation into the world of unskilled labour, so in general does the whole of the capitalist class, considered as a unit, derive *special* benefit from its special ownership of the machines, while the working class in general gets no more than a living. Therefore, not until the workers force the principle of the social ownership of machinery, etc., can they partake of the total product in proportion to their contribution; consequently, not till then could we say that machinery benefits society as a whole, for it is only under those conditions that society will *be a whole* in relation to such a question.

Is Happiness as an end in view morally justified? The moral, as we have demonstrated, is that which serves the *general* needs of any definite social group. If any person attains happiness by pursuing a course of action that serves those general needs, then, even though the pursuit of happiness be the end in view rather than the general good of his group, it is justified; in the reverse case it is not. The same remarks apply to a small group within a large and, therefore, more general group. Where an individual *thinks* his actions to be in the general interest, it might be necessary to restrain him by the general might, for his is a special case; for example, a religious fanatic whose revivalist tendencies make for insanity among his followers.

Is it desirable that all people should have good health? Here we have a question that may be taken as a type of many similarly silly questions, it is like asking " should all people be virtuous?" or " is education a good thing?" Such questions are so far removed in the abstract from their concrete bases (sense perceptions) that no intelligent answers can be given until we have first brought them down to earth as it were, and the only way to do this is to substitute some *practical* question for the one submitted, for if we say " yes " in answer to our original question the answer has no practical value, it tells us nothing as to how good health may be secured because there is no absolutely general viewpoint in such matters.

For the sake of argument, let us assume that it is in the general interest and, therefore, desirable that all people should have good health. To carry this desire into effect it would be necessary to enlist the services of doctors, nurses and all persons capable of curing others, and if the desire were attained these people would have no work, and, from their particular standpoint, such an end is not desirable, so what are we to do? Provide for them at the public expense? But, public provision for doctors and nurses involves taxation, and taxation can never be quite equitable, so now the practical question submitted in place of the original one takes this form (it might take other forms, all that is meant just here is that it must take a *practical form*) " is State payment and control of the medical faculty desirable," and, from the workers' standpoint, we might add " and should workers work for this through their political or other organisations " ?

From the standpoint of those of the medical and nursing fraternities who fear bad administration, undue interference on the part of authorities, etc., the answer is in the negative. From those who are already in good health, but who would have to contribute, the general answer would probably be the same. It would be unprofitable at this point to follow out all the conflicting interests involved, even were it possible; all we need notice is that no intelligent answer can be given without a *knowledge of the material conditions which, in communion with the senses, produce the sense perceptions from which the understanding derives its generalisation.* Regarding the workers' interest in such a question, they need not waste any time on it, for if it is decided before the advent of socialism it will be by the generalising of the common features of the conflicting interests to which we have just referred, and these are interests in which workers have no control. Under communism, State support and control of the medical service would, of course, be a foregone conclusion, because by that time the chief contradictions between the different interests, which are mainly financial, would have already been solved through the successive over-riding of special interests by an ever-widening general, and, therefore, there would be no reason to interfere with the administration and directive ability of those who know best how to manage their own special work.

Are Strikes Unreasonable? Once again! All ideas are brought into being by the understanding generalising sense perceptions. Assume some working men have sense perceptions of what seems to them bad conditions in the workshop (bad because they do not serve their *general* need). Each one has a generalisation of his own, the result of his own reasoning. By conferring with one another they pool the common features of their separate and small generalisations into one idea, a greater generalisation, by taking a vote. If the decision is to strike then evidently that decision is arrived at by the *general* reason of that particular group of persons, and consequently is reasonable. But if this body of men constitute only a small section of those engaged in the whole industry, and if the rest of the main body do not think them justified or wise in their decision, then that decision, though general and reasonable for the smaller body, becomes particular or special when regarded from the standpoint of the larger body, and, of course, unreasonable, though if the larger body uphold the decision of the smaller one it remains reasonable; this is from the point of view of the workers. But since strikes in these days always mean a blow at some section of the capitalist class, either in attack or defence, then, from the point of view of the general body of capitalists, strikes are always unreasonable, as witness their views in the Press.

The foregoing leads to the next question, for if the reasonable is that which is general within the limits of a certain group, and this general is determined by taking a vote, does it follow that majority decisions, though reasonable, are always right?

Are Majorities always Right? The findings of a majority, as we have said, are reasonable because they are the product of reasoning *in general* as opposed to the reasoning *in particular* of smaller groups or of individuals; but these findings are not right, or true, unless they correspond with reality *outside the mind;* for it is often the fact that majority decisions in relation to industrial conditions are mere mental combinations built up, it is true, from sense perceptions of real parts existing outside the mind, but which do not exist *as combinations* outside the mind. Such decisions are generalisations which it is anticipated will serve some general *need,* but if the decisions are found to be impracticable, the general needs are not served, which is only another way of saying that the generalisations are errors; *but it is only after the trial* that they are seen to be unreasonable, because it is only then that they are seen to be incorrect. In case we should think this to be a contradiction, let us remember that *after* the trial a new set of sense perceptions has become available and they necessarily alter the previous generalisation, so what was previously reasonable becomes unreasonable. It is important to remember that error results from combining too few factors as well as from combining too many.

Should Workers Serve on Trade Union Executives? The means to an end are justified provided the end is justified. Since capitalism has been proved to be immoral because it does not serve the general needs of all people, it follows that those members of executives who interest themselves in making capitalism run smoothly, for example, those who support Whitley councils, Douglas (or other) credit schemes, "increased production," craft distinctions, etc., are not serving the general needs, and, consequently, are acting immorally, whether they know it or not, "ignorance of the law is no defence." Therefore, workers should serve on trade union executives only when by doing so they can contribute anything that will develop the workers' organised might, the might that is needed to demonstrate their general morality; for example, any move towards the abandonment of craft distinctions, or advocating *and helping to carry out* an educational policy that is independent of capitalist class influence, viz., that kind known as Independent Working-Class Education, which deals with those branches of social science calculated to give workers the knowledge of the correct relations between themselves and their masters.

ABSTRACT AND CONCLUSION. We opened this introduction by demonstrating the need for a method of arriving at truth, and then outlined the evolution from nebula to man, in which took place the gradual development of organs of sense and brains. From sense perceptions of things not classified and, therefore, not understood, men instinctively generalised notions of religious practices, gods and mythological legends which later developed into the several great religions that are now very much on the wane; this was one great line of thought. The next, beginning six centuries before Christ, was that of philosophy, in which men took to the investigation of nature in their search for truth, but as the results were disappointing, inasmuch as everything was changing and consequently there seemed no hope of arriving at any permanent truth in nature, they turned to search for reality in the study of mind. It was a hopeless quest, but has been pursued up to the present time, though it is now waning and beginning to follow religion on the downward grade. The third and last great line of thinking is known as science, it began about six centuries ago by taking once more to the study of nature, and, due to the newer tools and possibilities of research, it has had a long line of brilliant successes. It shed its light on philosophy and drove philosophers to study *thinking* rather than the reality of mind as an entity; this move was finally completed by a method of dialectic logic, through the work of Joseph Dietzgen, who placed thinking on a level with all other science by discovering its general law— that of combining parts into wholes or the reverse; with the establishing of this law philosophy as such ceased to be, its place being taken by the " Science of Understanding.'

We now have a scientific method of attacking all problems, but, like all methods, it is no use without material upon which to work. This material, as far as the past is concerned, is to be found in historical study, and with regard to the present in the study of economics and allied subjects. The material is little use without the method, nor the method without the material; those who have any sense worth having will study both, for there are only two alternatives, one is to retire from discussion and become a social hermit, the other is to be a fool who opens his lips only to be held up to ridicule by the rising army of proletarian logicians. But in the hope that readers will not let the principles taught herein drop out of their minds as the book drops out of their hands, but will begin to apply them and so grow into the habit of thinking scientifically, we give one more example by describing this end as

THE BEGINNING.

BIBLIOGRAPHY

ALLEN, GRANT. *The Evolution of the Idea of God :* Watts and Co., London, 1908.

BAX, E. BELFORT. *The French Revolution :* Swan Sonnenschein, London, 1907.

BERGSON, HENRI. *Creative Evolution :* Macmillan and Co., London, 1911.

BÜCHNER, LUDWIG. *Force and Matter :* Trübner and Co., London, 1864.

BÜCHNER, L. *Last Words on Materialism :* Watts, London, 1901.

CARR, H. WILDON. *The Philosophy of Change :* T. C. and E. C. Jack, London.

CRAIK, W. W. *Outlines of Philosophic Logic :* Out of print.

D'HOLBACH. *The System of Nature :* Truelove, London, 1884.

DIETZGEN, JOSEPH. *The Positive Outcome of Philosophy :* Kerr, Chicago, 1906.

DIETZGEN, JOSEPH. *Philosophical Essays :* Kerr, Chicago, 1917.

ENGELS, F. *Landmarks of Scientific Socialism :* Kerr, Chicago, 1907.

ENGELS, F. *Feuerbach—The Roots of the Socialist Philosophy :* Kerr, Chicago, 1912.

ENGELS, F. *Socialism, Utopian and Scientific :* Swan Sonnenschein, London, 1907.

ENGELS, F. *Origin of the family :* Kerr, Chicago, 1910.

FAIRGRIEVE, JAMES. *Geography and World Power :* University of London Press, London, 1920.

HEGEL. *History of Philosophy :* Kegan Paul, London, 1892.

HOGARTH, D. G. *The Ancient East :* Home University Library, Williams and Norgate, London.

JARRETT, BEDE. *Mediaeval Socialism :* T. C. and E. C. Jack, London.

KAUTSKY. *Ethics and the Materialist Conception of History :* Kerr, Chicago, 1918.

BIBLIOGRAPHY

LEWES, G. H. *The History of Philosophy :*   Longmans, Green, London, 1871.

MCCABE, JOSEPH.   *Evolution from Nebula to Man :* Milner and Co., Manchester.

MARX, KARL. *Critique of Political Economy* (Preface) *:*   Kerr, Chicago, 1913.

MARX and ENGELS.   *Communist Manifesto :* S. L. Press, Glasgow.

MEILY, CLARENCE.   *Puritanism :* Kerr, Chicago.

MORGAN, LEWIS H.   *Ancient Society :* Kerr, Chicago.

PAUL, WILLIAM.   *The State ; its Origin and Function :* S. L. Press, Glasgow.

PLECHANOFF, GEORGE.   *Anarchism and Socialism :* Kerr, Chicago, 1918.

RUSSELL, BERTRAND.   *The Problems of Philosophy :* H. U. Library, Williams and Norgate, London, 1918.

WEBB, C. C. J.   *A History of Philosophy :* H. U. Library, Williams and Norgate, London.

INDEX

Abelard 53
Absolute, the . . 88-90, 91
Academy, the . . . 35
Academicians, the New . 47
Adaptation . . . 83
Agnosticism . . . 13
Albertus Magnus . . 60
Anaxagoras . . 28, 41
Anaximander . . . 27
Anaximenes . . . 27
Anselm . . . 53, 66
Antagonism of material interests . . 56-9
Antisthenes . . . 32
à posteriori ideas . . 76
à priori ideas . . 75, 84
Aquinas 55
Arabian Philosophy . . 54
Arcesilaus . . . 47
Aristippus . . . 32
Aristocles . . . 33
Aristotle 35-6, 37, 41, 55, 60, 61, 62, 82
Augustine . 44, 66, 113
Authority, appeal to . . 12
Averroes 54

Bacon, Francis. 61, 65, 70, 95, 102
Bacon, Roger . . 60, 101
Baer, Karl von . . 104
Bain 95
Beauty . . 83-4, 159
Bentham 96
Bergson . . 98-9, 117
Berkeley . . 71-2, 74
Boethius 52
Boyle 104

Brahma 42
Brain work . . 129-134
Broad Mind, the . . 13
Bruno, Giordano . . 62
Büchner 109
Butler 81

Carneades . . . 47
Cassiodorus . . . 51
Categorical imperative 80, 81, 83
Categories, Kantian . . 78
Causality, the problem of . 73
Cause and Effect . 140-2
Chattel slavery . . 26, 56
Christianity and Christians 43-6, 49, 55, 56, 59, 60
Civilisation, beginnings of 22-3
Clark 81
Columbus . . . 61
Comte . . . 61, 87
Confusion of Schoolmen 53-6, 58
Constitutive notions . 76-7
Copernicus . . . 61
Couéism 162
Cratylus 33
Creation, the . . . 49
Cudworth . . . 81
Cuvier 104
Cynics 32
Cyrenaics . . . 31-2

Dark Ages . . . 52
Darkness . . . 147
Darwin . . . 95, 104
Deduction . . 60, 101
Democracy . . . 170
Democritus . . . 37

189

INDEX

Descartes . 64-7, 73, 85, 102
Destiny v. Grace . . 44
Determinism, see Freedom.
Determinism and Education 175-6
D'Holbach . . . 106
Dialectics . 29, 30, 31, 89
Dialectic method 89-92, 93, 111
Dietzgen . . . 113, 185
Diogenes 32
Double standard of truth. 56
Dualism 85
Duns Scotus . 55, 69, 102

Ecstatic union with God . 48
Education . . 173-5
Effect . . . 140-1
Eleatics 29
Electron theory . 98, 105
Encyclopædists . . 106
End and Means 167-8, 173, 178, 184
Engels . . 93, 110, 111
Epicureanism . 38, 44, 47
Epicurus 38
Evil . . . 178-9
Evolution, inorganic 16-8
Evolution, organic . 18-21
Evolution, of societies 21-3

Feudalism . . . 57
Feuerbach . . 110-11
Fichte . . . 87-8
Force and Matter . 145-51
Force and Matter . 110
Freedom . . 82-3, 99
Freedom and Will . 160-2

Galileo 62
Geometry, principles of, not eternal . . . 144
Gilbert 62
God 163
God, the idea of one 25, 42
Grace of God . . 44
Gravity 145
Green, Thomas Hill . 96-7

Hamilton, Sir W. . . 87
Happiness, moral aspect of 180-1

Hartley 95
Harvey 104
Heat 146
Hegel . . . 89-93
Hegelians, Young . 93, 110
Heraclitus . . . 27
Hobbes . . 67, 95, 102
Holiness . . . 167-9
Humanitarian principles 171-3
Hume . 72-3, 74, 75, 81, 95
Hutcheson . . . 81
Hutton 104
Hypnotism . . . 162

Ideals 173
Ideas, association of 95, 96
Immortality . 83, 158-9
Inductive method . 60-1, 101
Innate ideas . . 69-70
Inquisition, the . . 62
Islamism . . . 54
I. W.—C. E. . . 174, 184

James, William . . 97
Jews . 24, 42-3, 45, 57
Johnson, Dr. . . . 72
Justinian . . . 54

Kant 73, 75-85, 86, 90, 92-93, 104, 108
Kepler 62
Knowledge . . 162-3

Laplace 104
Lavoisier 104
Leibnitz . . 68-9, 70, 74
Life 156-8
Life, principle of . 97
Light 146
Lippershey . . . 62
Locke . 69-71, 74, 95, 103
Logic . 36, 39, 52, 60, 122
Logic, philosophic 123-5, 134
Logic, philosophic, applied to mind and matter 126-37
Lyceum, the . . . 36

Machine production benefits of . . . 179-80

INDEX

Mahomet . . . 54
Majority decisions, rightness
   of . . . 183-4
Malebranche . . . 68
Mansel, H. L. . . . 87
Marx . . 93, 110, 111-2
Marx, quotation from 63, 113
Materialism . . 61, 86
Materialism, English 101-5
Materialism, French . 105-8
Materialism, German 108-10
Materialistic conception of
   History . . . 111-3
Materialists, "metaphysical" 110
Mathematicians, the . 30
Matter . 121-2, 136-7, 145
Mechanical conception of
   universe . . . 67
Mediator, the . . 45
Metaphysics . . 77-9
Mill, James . . . 95
Mill, John Stuart . 95-6
Mind . . 121-2, 134-5
Mind and Matter 36, 39, 85, 137
Moleschotte . . . 109
Monetary power . 58, 166
Monotheism, *see* God, the
   idea of one.
Morality . . 163-7, 177-8
Moral reflex . . 80-1
Motion 148
Mysticism . . . 48

Nature . . . 138-40
Nebular Theory . 16-7
Neoplatonists . 43, 44, 46-9
Newton 104
Nietzsche . . . 94-5
Nominalists . . 53, 55-6
Nothing 149
Noumenon . . . 76-7

Occam, William of . . 56
Occasionalism . . 67-8
Ontological argument 66, 90

Pantheism . . . 68
Parmenides . . . 28
Perfection . . 159-60

Pelagius 44
Phenomena . . 76, 84
Philo 47
Philosophers—defined . 15
Philosophy, Ancient schools of,
   29-30, 31, 37, 46-7
Philosophy, comparison of
   Ancient and Modern . 99
Philosophy, problems of 11-16
Physicists, the . . . 29
Plato 31, 32-5, 37, 49, 53, 66
Plotinus . . . 47-8
Porphyry . . . 49, 52
Power 149
Predicables, the . . 52
Price, Richard . . . 81
Priestly 104
Proclus 49
Psychologists, the empirical 95
Pyrrho 37
Pythagoras . . 27-8

Rationalism . . . 86
Realism . 53, 55, 97, 103-5
Reason, pure . . 79, 82
Reason, practical . . 80
Reasonable, the . 152-5
Regulative notions . 79, 81, 86
Reid 95
Relativity . . . 87
Renaissance . 54, 63, 71, 106
Revolution, French . 92-3
Revolution, German . 109
Right . . . 163-7
Roscellinus . . . 53
Rousseau 106

Scepticism . . 37, 44, 73
Sceptics . . . 30, 38
Scheele 104
Schelling . . . 88
Scholasticism and Scholastics
   52-3, 82
Schopenhauer . . 93-4
Science, positive . . 101
Scottish School . . 95
Sensational School . 105
   (*See also* Bacon, Hobbes,
   Locke).
Sense perceptions . . 130

INDEX

Shaftesbury . . . 81
Shaw, G. B. . . . 97
Silence 147
Smith, Adam . . . 81
Socialisation of property,
   limits of justification 176-8
Socrates . 31, 32, 33, 41, 49
Something . . . 149
Sophists 30
Sound 147
Space 144
Spencer, Herbert 61, 87, 96, 97
Spinoza . . . 68, 74, 82
Stewart, Dugald . . 95
Stillness 148
Stoicism . . . 38, 44
Stoics 38-9
Straightness . . 142-3
Strikes . . . 182-3
Substitution of practical
   questions for abstract
   ones . . . 181-2
Superman, the doctrine of . 95
Synthetic philosophy . 97
System of Nature, The,
   argument in . . 106-7

Teleology . . . 28
Telescope, inventor and
   date of 62
Thales 26
Theology . . . 43
Thought . . . 129-30
Time 144
Time and Freewill . 98-9

Time, the essence of reality 98-9
Tithes 57
Trade Union Executives,
   morality of serving on . 184
Trinity, the Alexandrian . 48
Trinity, the Christian 46, 53
Truth and Error . . 152
Truth, method of finding 132-4

Unit, the mathematical 143-4
Universe, parts of the 127-8
Unnatural, the . 139-40
Urea, synthetic . . 104
Usury . . . 58, 166
Utilitarianism . . . 96
Utopians and Utopianism—
   Ancient . . . 113
   Mediaeval . . 113-4
   Modern . . 114-6

Vedism 42
Vesalius 62
Vogt, Carl . . . 109
Voltaire 106

Will, the freedom of the
                44, 68, 82
William of Champeaux . 56
" Will to live," the . . 94
Wöhler 104
" Word," the . . . 47

Zeno (of Elea, dialectician). 29
Zeno (Stoic) . . . 38
Zoroaster 42

Printed in Great Britain by C. TINLING & Co., LTD.,
53, Victoria Street, Liverpool,
and at London and Prescot

UNIVERSITY OF CALIFORNIA LIBRARY
Los Angeles
This book is DUE on the last date stamped below.

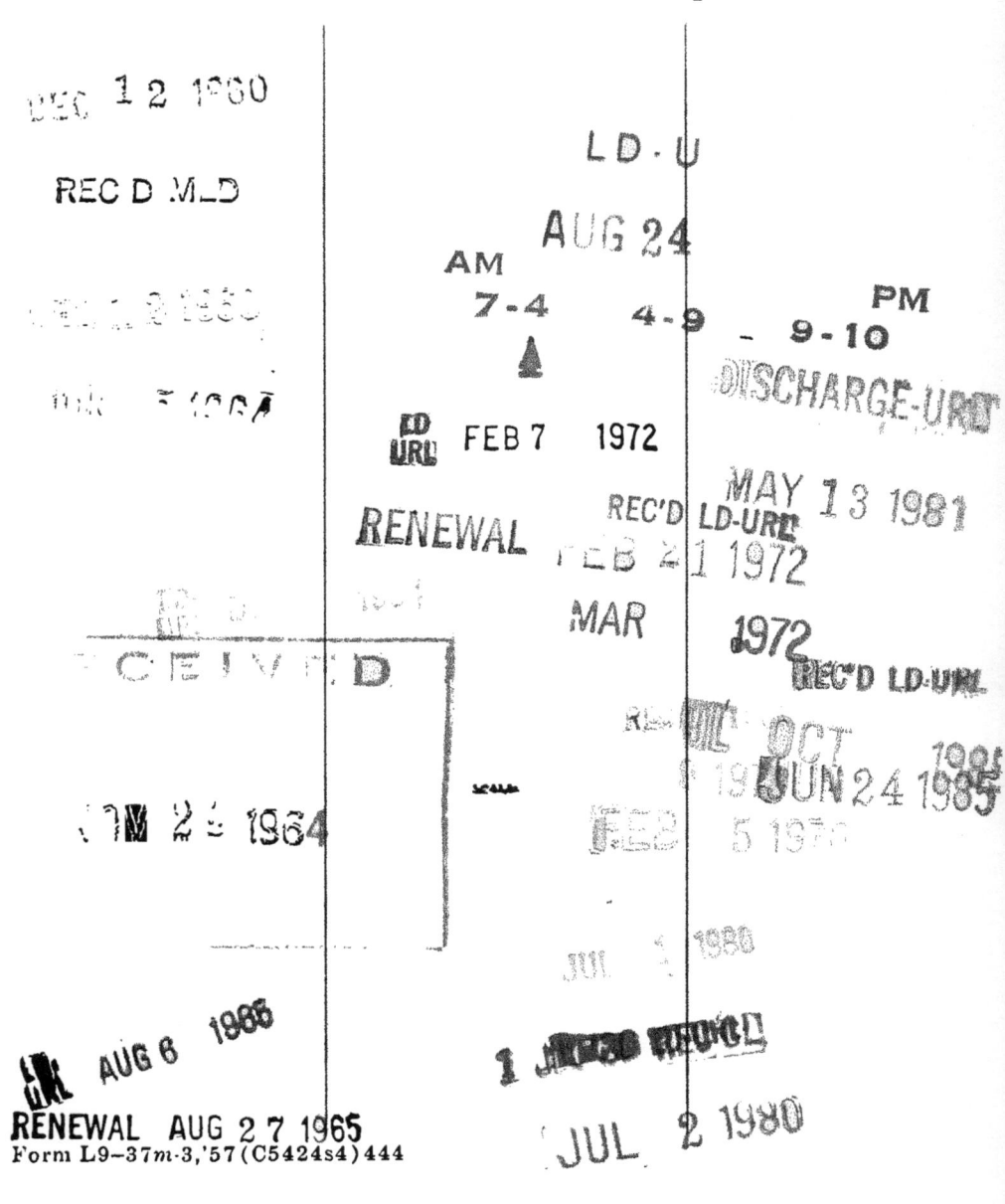

Form L9–37m-3,'57(C5424s4)444

Lightning Source UK Ltd.
Milton Keynes UK
UKHW02f0748030818
326718UK00008B/432/P